What Drowns the Flowers in Your Mouth

LIVING OUT

Gay and Lesbian Autobiographies

David Bergman, Joan Larkin, and Raphael Kadushin
FOUNDING EDITORS

WHAT DROWNS THE FLOWERS IN YOUR MOUTH

A Memoir of Brotherhood

Rigoberto
González

THE UNIVERSITY OF WISCONSIN PRESS

Publication of this book has been made possible, in part,
through support from the **Brittingham Trust.**

The University of Wisconsin Press
1930 Monroe Street, 3rd Floor
Madison, Wisconsin 53711-2059
uwpress.wisc.edu

3 Henrietta Street, Covent Garden
London WCE 8LU, United Kingdom
eurospanbookstore.com

Printed in the United States of America

This book may be available in a digital edition.

Library of Congress Cataloging-in-Publication Data

Names: González, Rigoberto, author.
Title: What drowns the flowers in your mouth: a memoir of brotherhood /
Rigoberto González.
Other titles: Living out.
Description: Madison, Wisconsin: The University of Wisconsin Press, [2018]
| Series: Living out: gay and lesbian autobiographies
Identifiers: LCCN 2017042900 | ISBN 9780299316907 (cloth: alk. paper)
Subjects: LCSH: González, Rigoberto—Family. | Authors,
American—20th century—Biography. | Mexican
American gays—Biography.
Classification: LCC PS3557.O4695 Z46 2018 | DDC 813/.54 [B]—dc23
LC record available at https://lccn.loc.gov/2017042900

For
Turrútut

Contents

What Drowns the Flowers in Your Mouth

Opening Salvo

The two earliest moments I recall being aware of my younger brother take me back to Zacapu, Michoacán, in the mid-1970s. In the first, I'm playing with aluminum toys on the kitchen floor while my mother stands in front of the stove. The sharp corners on the miniature truck keep me focused on the task at hand: creating small collisions as I flutter my lips for effect. I remember my mother's legs underneath a dress, which seems odd because in most of my childhood memories, I picture my mother wearing pants. The dresses I associate with her are hospital gowns, the ones she wore during her quick decline in the 1980s, shortly before her death. But in that memory, she's full of life and inhabiting a domestic scene that made me feel safe and cared for. Our home, so sturdy and large. My mother, always within reach. I remain distracted by my childish game until I'm startled by a gurgling above. I look up. It's a small body locked inside a high chair, banging a plate on the plastic tray before him. He's a funny-looking thing—a pale animal with stumpy limbs making awkward sounds like a wounded bird. I stare at him for a few seconds, trying to figure out who brought this into the house and for what purpose. When my mother turns around and puts food in his tiny mouth, I recognize that he's here to stay, that he will compete with me for attention and affection, and since he's clearly more helpless than me, I'm going to be asked to keep him company. My resentment grows. He's going to be a lot of work, this one. But just as quickly,

3

so does my excitement intensify. There are two of us now. And that's like being twice as big, twice as strong, twice as fun. I will teach him. I will lead the way.

The second moment is more vivid. It's rainy season, and the clouds over Zacapu are moody. At any moment, they release their heavy drops over the town, sparing nothing and no one. That's how my little brother gets caught in the downpour just outside the house. He stands frozen, holding on to his bicycle with training wheels, crying for help. My mother shakes her head as she hands me an umbrella and tells me to bring him in. This gives me a sense of superiority. Not only did I make it home because I gauged the arrival of the rain better than he did, but I had to go back out to rescue him. I pop open the umbrella and walk through the garden, the rain getting louder as it strikes the foliage harder. I open the front gate, its squeak muffled by the noisy weather. When he sees me coming, my brother amplifies his wailing. I shield him immediately and then walk him into the haven of the house, my hand on his soaked back, prodding him forward. "Don't worry, Alex," I say. "I'm here now."

Of those two moments, it's the second that flushed into my brain when I received an unexpected phone call from México. It was Guadalupe, my sister-in-law. I was in Montpelier, Vermont, at a writers' conference in the summer of 2010. I was strolling absent-mindedly in the peaceful afternoon sun when Guadalupe informed me that my brother, living on the Mexican border town of Mexicali, had been kidnapped. I froze, my feet anchored to the earth as my head spun in circles while I came to terms with the helplessness of the situation. What could I do from so far away? What could I advise except to mutter words that I never imagined would ever come out of my mouth: "When they ask for a ransom, tell me," I told my sister-in-law. "I will pay it. I'll pay anything." When she burst into tears, I became aware of how surreal it was to be connected to such a scenario through my cell phone while standing in Montpelier with its sky so clear and so clean, its light so bright.

And then my body temperature changed and everything around me darkened with shadow.

While I waited to hear back from my sister-in-law, I kept my body locked in place, afraid that if I moved, she wouldn't find me again. My body shook but I couldn't cry—there was so much uncertainty about the situation, I thought it would be premature to do so. Instead, I imagined the terrible price that was going to be placed on my brother's life, and tried to determine if I could actually pay it with my paltry savings account and no other family I could reach out to. At that moment, I felt like a failure; I had failed my parents because I had failed to protect my little brother. Eventually I arrived at the most horrific outcome: whether or not I could actually gather the funds, would my brother be allowed to live? I had heard too many heartbreaking stories about my beloved homeland's current crisis to have much hope: toes and ears delivered to family members who delayed payment, decapitated bodies to those families that didn't manage to pay, and even to those that did. But other than that, I had no context for what was happening to us. We were not wealthy Mexicans, though that didn't matter anymore—anyone was vulnerable. I suspected that my brother had been targeted because he owned a small business making tacos. It was his dream to have a little side business, and I had helped fund it from afar, thinking that I had done something good for my little brother to help him get ahead. But now, there I was, cold, clammy, and probably responsible for my own brother's abduction. If I lost my brother, I would have no one. Our mother was dead. Our father was dead. To lose my brother would be so unfair after all my other losses.

As I waited for that second call from Guadalupe, I gathered what I could remember about my relationship with my brother, about the ways in which our journeys followed the same path and the ways in which they never intersected. I tried to piece together again the story of our lives as men because everything inside me had just shattered.

Days of Hunger, Days of Want

The season of scrambled eggs came upon us on January 6, Three Kings Day. Perhaps it was the holiday spirit—the gifts, the piñata, the candy—that reminded my mother's younger sisters that it was time to start planning for Holy Week, only three months away. Their appeal, made just when the day's excitement quieted down over dinner, made my body stiffen because it was an announcement of the labor to come.

"Don't forget, everybody," Tía Luz said. "Start saving eggshells."

"Please," Tía Chata added. She resembled my mother the most because they were both short and had the same pale skin. Tía Luz was the youngest, but also the tallest, and she always sported the same shoulder-length hairdo.

A few heads nodded in acknowledgment, and this seemed to satisfy my aunts. The evening's meal progressed as if nothing had changed, but in fact, it had changed breakfast every morning. No more hard-boiled eggs or eggs served sunny-side up until enough shells had been collected for the cascarón sale. My fingers twitched because they still carried the memory of the times the sharp edges pricked their tips.

On the way home, I held my bag of candy, too distracted to eat more of it. My mother walked in front of me with a plastic bag over her shoulder, my toys inside. I pictured her in the kitchen, tapping the end of the egg in order to make an opening large enough to coax the contents out yet small enough to ensure that the egg preserved its oval shape. Once we had enough of them, my aunts would come over with the art supplies: scissors and construction paper to make the confetti that would be stuffed inside the shell, thin tissue paper to glue over the opening, and food coloring to paint the shells pink or blue or green. Each of the tasks demanded patience and skill that I was too young to handle, but my aunts insisted—cascarones were an Alcalá family tradition, and although I was actually a González first, I was the oldest grandchild on the Alcalá side. My brother, Alex, was only a year and a half younger, but he was still considered too clumsy to handle the delicate task of making a cascarón. My father had objected in the beginning, on the grounds that this was woman's labor, but my mother didn't take long to remind him that until I became a man, I was under the care of the Alcalá women, who seemed to come around too often and stayed too long—or so I heard my father mumble many times.

Making cascarones was just one of the Alcalá women enterprises. In the summers, they made bolis (flavored ice), in August they made paper doves for the church's celebration of the Virgin Mary, and in the winters they made tamales and champurrado, a hot cornmeal drink. All these items they sold from the living room or at the town plaza, where the citizens of Zacapu converged in the evenings, particularly before and after church. My aunts sometimes made commemorative keepsakes for birthday parties and weddings and brought over the materials to our house then too. I half-listened to them giggling and gossiping with my mother while I played at their feet. They didn't ask me to be part of the circle of bodies around the kitchen table, and I didn't miss it. I knew my time would come, and when it did, I wouldn't like it.

What was more maddening than cutting paper into tiny little pieces to make confetti and then sticking them into the tiny little holes, which is how I hurt myself on the pointy edges, was adding the signature detail to the Alcalá cascarones: at the intact tip of the eggshell, I would have to dab a little drop of glue and then sprinkle just the smallest amount of glitter. Many of the clients who bought cascarones missed this detail because they were so anxious to break them on top of someone's head—which is why they had been made in the first place. No one held the cascarón in his hand and admired the artistry, the tell-tale signs that this was an Alcalá cascarón, not just one of those sloppy ones that had been assembled in a rush. That was what upset me most of all: that it took so long to make one of these, and in one fell swoop it was gone—turned into rubbish in an instant.

I once started to color an eggshell, and Tía Luz ordered me to stop immediately.

"Why?" I asked.

"The opening is too large," she explained. "Throw it away."

"Who's going to notice?" I said.

"We will. It's going to look vulgar and cheap. We don't make vulgar and cheap."

I looked closer at the opening. Compared to all the others, this one looked like the egg had been cut in half, not carefully tapped open by my mother's hands. The tissue covering would have to be wide. More glue would have to be used. She was right. It was going to look vulgar and cheap. I set it aside and moved on to another, which now looked elegant with its smaller opening.

As my little brother struggled in my father's arms, weary and bored after another long visit to our relatives on the opposite side of town, I swelled with pride that I had a part to play and that it would set me apart from the moody child annoying my parents on the walk back home. And though I still wasn't looking forward to months of scrambled eggs, I was more comfortable with the idea.

"Don't forget about the eggshells, Mami," I said.

My father scoffed, and my mother gave him a friendly swat on the arm.

"You'll have to remind me again at breakfast," my mother said.

By the time we got to the house, I had all but convinced myself that I couldn't wait to make cascarones.

A few weeks passed, and the eggshells were accumulating in a small box next to the stove. I caught a glimpse of it once in a while as I played near my mother when she was cooking. When my aunts arrived, they always entered without knocking, so I was always caught off guard when the front door suddenly flew open and they burst in with their art supplies.

"We've got a cute order, Avelina; wait until you see this," Tía Chata said.

"I'll help you mop so that you can sit down with us," Tía Luz said.

And in no time, the three sisters were sitting around the table, giggling and gossiping like usual.

This time, however, my mother brought the reverie to a halt when she made an announcement about my father that made even me stop to listen.

"Rigoberto's going to the north to work," my mother said.

"Really?" Tía Chata said. "Leaving you and the babies all alone?"

I only became the baby when someone wanted to highlight my vulnerability. At six years old, with a bicycle that had no training wheels, I hardly felt like a baby anymore. My little brother, Alex, who still ate from a high chair, was the baby.

"Do you want one of us to move in with you to keep you company?" Tía Luz suggested. But I knew even then that this would never happen. If my father barely tolerated the long visits by my mother's family, he would definitely not put up with any of them moving in. It wasn't so much his objection but pressure from the González side of the family, who didn't seem to take a liking to the Alcalás—they were too religious and too forthright. The Gonzálezes were drinkers and partiers.

"I'll be fine," my mother said. "It's better this way." And we all knew what she meant.

In the coming weeks, I didn't really notice my father's absence too much, perhaps because I rarely spent any time with him. Once in a while, I would dream about him and casually ask my mother where he was and what he was doing.

"Working," is all she would answer.

What I did notice was that my aunts stopped coming around. Suddenly the house appeared too empty and quiet without their laughter. When I asked about them, my mother would look away and make some dismissive remark. But most noticeable of all was that we had stopped having eggs for breakfast. My mother started feeding me farina, which I didn't like much because it tasted gooey and grainy.

"I want eggs," I said to her in protest one morning. And so my mother burst into tears.

I didn't know how to respond. So I ate my farina without further complaints, and each morning after that I was careful not to let her see how displeased I was with my breakfast. I caught a glimpse of the box of eggshells and thought longingly about those days when the dreaded scrambled eggs graced my plate. What I wouldn't give to have them again.

And then the farina ran out and I longed for it as well because now my mother was feeding me tortillas with salsa.

I understood the word "poverty" but I had never experienced hunger. I didn't realize they came hand in hand. At school, I recognized children who had less than I did. I could tell by their shoes, their notebooks, which were always smaller than mine. But I also recognized children who had shinier shoes than I did and who carried notebooks that were thicker and heavier. Suddenly it made sense why my aunts and my mother would gather to make their arts and crafts—they were not just entertainment or excuses to socialize; these were economic necessities, proper ways for God-fearing women to make a little extra money. All those coins in the can they brought back from the plaza paid for staples like bread and milk. And eggs. Now that my aunts were not coming around for some inexplicable reason, now that my father was gone, it was just my mother, my baby brother, and me, consuming very little or nothing at all. And when something is gone, it is eventually forgotten and no longer missed.

A group of boys started playing marbles in front of the house one afternoon after school, and that was my cue to run into my room to grab my cache. I eased my way into the next round. I played with my lucky white cat's eye, which the other boys coveted. Halfway into the game, one of them wanted it badly enough to cheat, so I called him on it.

"I'm not cheating," he said. "The cat's eye is mine now."

"You leaned in too far," I said. "You didn't shoot behind the line."

"Yes, I did," he insisted.

I picked up my cat's eye and pocketed it. "I'm not letting it go."

"Oh, now who's the one cheating?"

The other boys didn't step in to defend either one of us. This was the law of the game. Contentious calls had to be resolved by the two parties involved. I held my stance, remaining motionless until his next move, which seemed to be evidence enough of my accusation because the boy withdrew, but not before letting out a cruel remark.

"I'm letting you have it," he said. "Because your father left you."

I looked around at the other faces. They seemed to be complicit in this knowledge that up until that moment I didn't have. I heard someone laugh, a giggle that might have been prompted by the most unrelated reason to what had just been revealed, but at that moment I felt the sting of ridicule. Red-faced, I ran into the house. By the time I reached my mother, I was in tears.

"What happened?" she said. "Did someone hit you?"

"Where's my father? Did he leave us? Did he really leave us?"

My mother's eyes began to water. She had this devastating ability to cry instantly, and it bothered me because that excused her from verbalizing her pain, from offering no more than an emotional response. There was nowhere to go but into silence after that. I was six years old. What did I have to know about our broken home except that it was now as empty as my stomach, something else to get used to?

Alex appeared clueless about our predicament. He walked around the house in that turtleneck sweater that he refused to take off even though Mami kept asking him to. With the rainy season came the oppressive humidity. I wondered if his thin, tiny frame even felt hunger the way my body did. Sometimes I would stare at him with envy, his peace left undisturbed by his lack of understanding that our mother had hidden us away in shame. Other times, I was grateful that at least one person was spared the terrible truths that weighed over the rest of us. If my mother discreetly moved food from her plate onto mine, I would do the same with my brother's plate when she wasn't looking. My brother received the offering passively and without objection, as if he sensed somehow that this was the new dynamic at the dining table. At night, Mami would light a candle in front of a picture of Jesus and we would pray together, and I marveled at the strength it took for God to hear such pleas and do nothing. Every night, we performed the same ceremony. I grew thinner, but my body appeared to be sinking into the mattress. I imagined that months later the bed would swallow me completely.

Then one day, miraculously, my father reappeared, dark and handsome as always. I wasn't sure how much time had passed since he had vanished—a few weeks, maybe a few months—though long enough for me to push him out of my mind. And suddenly there he was, smiling down at me as if he had only gone to town for a quick errand. And just as easily as I had forgotten him, I remembered him, pleased that his absence could not be used against me on the streets or at school. My mother must have felt the same because she paraded him down the block, their arms locked, for all the neighbors to see. Even the kitchen went back to normal. Even my breakfast plate because there, glorious as gold, were my scrambled eggs again.

No one mentioned my father's disappearance or subsequent reappearance—not in front of me anyway, and I didn't ask about it. The more it remained unsaid, the more it became undone, this painful period of my childhood. And cascarón season came to a close with a successful sale at the plaza during Holy Week. It seemed everything was back in its place, and I even set a few cascarones aside for myself, which I had never done before. I broke one on my father's head, and he laughed as the confetti rained over him. I gave him my second one and he broke it over my mother's head. At the end of the night, Alex slept soundly over my father's shoulder as I fought drowsiness to watch the highlight of the festivities—the burning of El Castillo de Chuchurumbé, an intricate fire-works structure with fire wheels and sparklers that was all whistles and explosions, a castle that shrieked and cried so that we didn't have to.

But if happiness had come back to our house, it didn't last long. Four years later, the González family was living in California, squeezed into a single house with my grandparents, my uncle's family, and my aunt's—nineteen bodies in one tiny space—a complete shift from our household arrangement in México, where the possibility of having Tía Luz or Tía Chata move in with us for a spell was not even an option. But as usual, there was no questioning the why or how of things; there was just surrender and moving forward with the decisions of the grown-ups.

The biggest challenge was getting used to living with Abuelo—and his bristly mustache—who always seemed annoyed and angry. As the patriarch, he kept a close eye on the goings on in the house, particularly in the kitchen, which he had claimed as his domain above all the women because, in a poor household, whoever controlled the food controlled the family. If he wasn't snapping at the women over their wasteful cooking habits, he was yelling at any of the kids who dared wander to the refrigerator uninvited. He was like the guard dog that instills such fear that he's even scarier when he's not in sight.

Unlike my older cousins, I was having an easier time adapting, probably because at ten years old, I enjoyed school and learning English. One of my first friendships was with a girl named Eve. She was half Panamanian, and her mother spoke fluent Spanish, but Eve was monolingual. She also had a small dog, named Peanut, which they kept in her backyard.

One summer, Eve went on vacation with her family, so she enlisted me to feed Peanut once a day. All I had to do was unlatch the gate, scoop half a can of dog food into the plastic dish, and fill the second dish with fresh water. I accepted the responsibility, not because I cared much for Peanut, who barked too much, but because I liked the idea of a pet. We had dogs in México, but they had functions—to guard the house from the rooftop—while Peanut was a fat little critter that couldn't even guard her own dish. It was an entirely different relationship with animals that intrigued me, yet I had no fantasies that we would ever have a pet, and we never did at that address.

Eve gave me an opened can, and Eve's father gave me money to buy more dog food later in the week. I waved at the family as they drove away, and then I sauntered back home. I announced to everyone in the kitchen that I would be storing the dog food in the refrigerator, and no one batted an eye.

A few days later, Abuelo opened the refrigerator and asked

about the can. I explained my role as animal caretaker, and he simply shrugged.

"What's it made of?" he asked, inspecting the can.

I was surprised by the question. "Meat, I guess," I said. I read the ingredients more closely and translated what little I could.

"Meat," Abuelo repeated. He placed the can back into refrigerator and went about his day. So did I.

The next time I took a can over to Eve's house, I became curious about the dog food. It didn't smell like any meat I had ever tasted, but this was the U.S., and there were foods here I had never smelled or eaten before. As Peanut ate her fill, I dared to take a pinch of food out of the can and place it into my mouth. I didn't swallow it, but the taste lingered even after I spat it out. My curiosity satisfied, I knew I would never do that again, yet I still blushed, embarrassed at my own bravado.

Months later, as Christmas season approached, I recognized something familiar was happening in the kitchen. I knew that hollow sound of pots and pans ringing without purpose, of the refrigerator light glaring at its ribs, of the desperation in the voices of the grown-ups as they fought over supplies to feed their young. For dinner, Abuelo cooked these greasy stews that filled us up with hot oily water, but later that night my mother called my brother and me into her bedroom, and she sneaked a slice of Spam into our mouths. On those occasions, I only pretended to brush my teeth. I looked forward to going to bed with that taste locked in my mouth, swirling my tongue around and around until sleep defeated me.

School lunch was another reason to look forward to school days, and I don't remember if we were coached or not, but we didn't reveal to anyone that we showed up without having breakfast. This poverty was temporary—that's what we were told at home. No sense letting anyone else in on our shame. It was the same silence we had to keep about how many people were actually living at home. Since many of us were undocumented, we didn't want to invite any scrutiny from neighbors, teachers, post office workers—any one of them was a phone call away from the immigration authorities. We allowed no one to look in, and we certainly didn't leak anything out.

At about this time, Abuela started feeding us vitamins, huge red pills the size of a toy car—or so we joked. It was also a thing of humor to stand in a line with my brother and my eight cousins, each one of us taking our turn as Abuela shoved that monster pill down our throats. "Don't choke, don't choke!" the others chanted as Abuela made sure the pill was swallowed.

The grown-ups must have worked hard to protect us children from really seeing what was happening in that household. If my older cousins understood, they didn't share it with us younger ones. I figured it out because I had been down this road before, and so I also went to lengths to keep my knowledge a secret from those younger than I.

One evening, Abuelo prepared a casserole he called lasagna. It was an Italian dish, he bragged, and he was particularly proud of this because he used the oven, which was a feature of the stove none of the women in the family had occasion to operate.

As we gathered in the living room to watch TV, a smell wafted among us that made our mouths water. I thought that perhaps this might be the turning point we had all been waiting for, the sign of better times to come. It was customary for the children to eat first, so all ten of us squeezed around the table to receive a serving of this fancy lasagna dish Abuelo had made.

I didn't admit it to myself at first, but there was a familiar smell on my plate. I couldn't quite place it, so I thought that perhaps it was my mind reaching back to a flavor I had not had the pleasure of enjoying since the kitchen went bare. But when I took the first bite, I remembered: it was Peanut's food from the can. The others didn't know this. Their responses to the food were mixed. Some took a few bites and then started to eat around the meat, and others ate the meat willingly. It was lasagna, it was Italian food, it was supposed to taste funny. But the pasta was soft and the tomato sauce was tasty. It would do.

The sound of chewing around me was deafening, and it took me back to that moment I had experienced hunger once before, when my father had disappeared. Suddenly it all came back to me—how it felt as if my guts were tying knots around each other, how I came across a candle on my mother's bureau, the one that released the scent of cinnamon, and how I couldn't figure out how those teeth marks had gotten there, but now I did. I had always heard the grown-ups say that I would never be able to tell when my body was stretching because it happened gradually. But something inside me grew in an instant and I felt like exploding.

Abuelo stood at a distance, rubbing his mustache. His face appeared pleased somehow, maybe curious about how effectively he had deceived us. I wanted to detect some cruelty in his gesture, but I didn't find any. Instead, I saw sadness in its pure form for the very first time. It was a look of defeat, as if he had wanted us to reject this food, to spit it out and cry foul, to accuse him with fits of anger that he had fed us dog food. It would be a moment of truth for all of us, to finally admit that this moving from one country to another had not solved our problems, had not delivered on a promise to lift us out of poverty, to satiate our hunger. And that would have meant that all this sacrifice, all this hope we had packed into our bags, all this hiding and secret-keeping, had been for nothing. I could tear this whole theater apart and end the dream for all of us, or I could triumph over the test that had been set before me. Eat it or beat it back to México.

"Are you going to eat your food?" Alex asked.

I looked down at my plate. I had scarcely touched it. My fork was still buried in the entrails of the dog food lasagna. The moment of reckoning was in my hands. I was no longer the boy who belonged to the Alcalá women; I was now a young man who had joined the hardscrabble lives of the González family. And so had my little brother, who ate the lasagna with a sense of urgency. Without further hesitation, I scooped out a generous portion of the lasagna and stuffed it into my mouth.

The Prisoner
of Nahuatzen

Despite the meaning of its name, "place where it frosts," on the few occasions I visited Nahuatzen, the weather was muggy and humid. The first time, I must have been thirteen going on fourteen. Each summer, my paternal grandparents took a road trip to México to visit relatives and deliver clothing they had been gathering all year from the flea markets. They took turns taking one of their grandchildren with them, but after my mother passed away, they became my legal guardians, and so thereafter my brother, Alex, and I made the trips down with them. Eventually, even Alex tired of the two-day drive in the back of a truck, *pirekuas* playing at full volume, and I made the journey all alone under the camper, sleeping and daydreaming, except when we made brief stops to stretch our legs.

On one occasion, as we entered the state of Michoacán, we stopped in Nahuatzen. It was a surprising decision—the first time we had ever done so. I could tell by the way Abuela María became emotional. This was the place of her birth. To me, it was a town like all the others: mud buildings stood next to cement ones; a Pepsi logo painting on the side of one structure let it be known it was the store; uneven sidewalks flanked the cobblestone street; stray dogs walked past; and citizens of the town milled about, usually men in worn hats turning their heads whenever a vehicle drove by.

Abuelo pulled up next to a kiosk in the town square. Every town had a zócalo, large or small. This one was a tinier version of the ones I had grown up with in Zacapu, before my family uprooted and moved to California, before we traded the wide, open space of a town square for the cramped living rooms of our homes in the U.S.

I was about to hop off the back when my grandfather stopped me.

"Don't bother," he snapped, banging the side of the truck with his fist. "We're not staying here long."

I looked over at Abuela María. She already knew this and couldn't hide the look of disappointment on her face. I said nothing and sat back down. Abuelo left the camper door open, fortunately, and so I was able to look out at the people looking back at me.

"Pardon me, friends," my grandfather said to a pair of men nearby. "Where can I buy music in this town?"

The question disarmed the men, who had been considering us apprehensively. They knew by our clothing we were not from around here. My grandfather sported a crisp new hat he only wore on his visits to México. My grandmother had short, dyed hair—an unusual look for an older woman in these parts.

The men pointed to a building just across the zócalo. I was tempted to spring out of the camper as soon as my grandfather walked into the building, but I knew better than to disobey him. Abuela María sat in the truck cabin and took in whatever she could from where we were parked. It was hot, and I was grateful that Abuela María walked over to the little store to bring me a *jarrito*, a tamarind-flavored soda. I knew the drill. I finished the drink quickly and then handed back the bottle, which Abuela returned to the grocer to get her cash deposit back.

"Do you recognize anyone?" I asked Abuela after she came back from the store.

"Nothing but strangers in this town," she said heavily, and I wasn't sure if she was referring to us or to the people on the square.

Abuela climbed into the front of the truck. To demonstrate my empathy, I wanted to mutter the few words in Purépecha she had taught me, but they had flown right out of my head. This failure saddened me even more.

As I savored the dissolving flavor of tamarind, I considered the way Abuelo became extraordinarily meek when he interacted with others. It never ceased to annoy me because I knew his true temperament—he was mean-spirited and unnecessarily cruel. That soft voice turned disdainful as soon as the person he was talking to was out of earshot. He had to show his true colors to us, those who lived with him; otherwise we could not fear him.

I knew this surprise visit to Nahuatzen was some sort of torture he was inflicting on my grandmother, showing her something she couldn't have. I imagined she still had relatives there, and old friendships with old stories she wished to hear again or be reminded of. But at least she felt the ground beneath her feet, and her entire body took in the breeze. I sat quietly in the back of the truck the entire time like a caged bird without a song.

Just then, a young man around my age rolled over in an old bicycle. The paint had chipped all over the metal body, and the handlebars were missing the rubber grips. Someone had wrapped cloth around the handlebars to protect his hands from blistering. I recalled such blistered hands from my Mexican neighborhood so many years ago. He was curious and fearless about approaching me.

"You're from the north?" he asked, pointing with his chin. He placed one hand on the tailgate to keep his balance as he swayed back and forth. I sensed the two men quiet down to eavesdrop.

"Yes," I said. "From California."

He looked inside the camper. There was nothing much to see, only the garbage bags filled with clothes that I leaned against when I slept. Our luggage was stacked in one corner. I brought nothing more than a duffel bag.

"You bring any marbles from the north?"

I was caught off guard by the question. I remembered those toys from childhood: marbles, a top, a yo-yo, a slingshot, a balero—the cup-and-ball game I never mastered. I owned none of these anymore and I couldn't explain to myself why not. How did they not cross the border with me? How did they disappear from my list of things that brought me joy? And what had replaced them?

"No. I don't play marbles," I admitted.

The young man laughed incredulously. "Really?"

I knew I had become even more foreign to him, and this brought me some shame. But there was no way to convince him that deep down inside I was just like him, a Michoacano—of Purépecha bloodlines with ties to Nahuatzen, the very place we now breathed in. There was my proof sitting in the truck. I turned around and tried to find my grandmother in the cabin. But the camper wall obstructed my view.

Suddenly I felt the young man's finger brush across my wrist. Up until that sensation, I had not realized that I too had my hand resting on the tailgate. He remained expressionless, as if that was enough to hide the breach of boundary even from me. The old men behind him did not suspect anything. It appeared that they had lost interest in the visitors from the north entirely and weren't even looking our way. The young man, meanwhile, continued to roll back and forth, back and forth, and the motion became somewhat erotic for me. I still felt his touch on my skin, and now it burned even more.

"What is your name?" I asked.

He grinned, looking shy suddenly. "I'm not going to give you my name."

He said this flirtatiously, and I wasn't sure how to interpret it. Was he mocking me, or was he revealing something about himself only to me? A quiet came over us as if we were communicating telepathically, and this comforted me. It gave me courage to move my hand on the tailgate a few inches toward his. I was imagining myself daring to shift my fingers even closer when he broke the trance.

"Give me *your* name," he said.

The way his eyelashes fluttered when he said that gave him away: he had seen right through me and was now going to use that knowledge against me. I had been through this so many times before in both México and the U.S.—a young man would coax that hidden part of me out into the open and then stomp on it. It was the part of me that made me vulnerable no matter where I lived, no matter where I went.

Without moving, I felt myself withdraw into myself. The cave of the camper became darker, and I wanted to vanish inside of it. My look of hurt, of disappointment, was also a strategy, though it didn't always work, but when it did, my tormentor would take pity on me and drop his game. This time, the moment was interrupted by my grandfather's return. He arrived holding a few cassette tapes, and with his free hand, he reached up to grab the camper door.

"Excuse me, boy," Abuelo said. His voice sounded so kind and feminine that it made me angry. The one time I might have excused my grandfather's rudeness, that acidic tongue he used on me too often was not there.

The young man rolled out of the way as my grandfather closed the door on me, and I was again protected inside. A minute later, we were on the road once more, headed for Zacapu. Abuelo tested one of the tapes. The speakers were latched to the inside of the camper, which is why my grandparents turned the volume up, high enough so that they could hear from the cabin. I was locked inside with the violins and guitars, the high-pitched *pirekua* singers, no Purépecha vocabulary and no marbles in my pocket. I saw the young man through the small back window, and I forgave him because he had less than I did, and I had the luxury of summer travel, clean American clothes, and, if I really wanted them, toys, shiny and new. And yet I envied him because on his rusty old bicycle, he could be himself because, unlike me, he was undeniably free.

ADELINA'S STORY

The summer after we moved in with my grandparents, the idea was born to bring back "una muchacha"—a young woman—from México. The purpose was to find a caretaker for my father, recently widowed, and a nanny for my brother and me, recently orphaned at ages ten and twelve. Abuela, the only female in the small two-bedroom cinderblock apartment, had become exhausted managing a household that had doubled overnight. It seemed like a good solution, though I couldn't imagine where they were thinking of housing this seventh body. My grandparents slept in one bedroom; my father, my brother, and my bachelor uncle slept in the other. I slept on the couch in the tiny living room. This didn't bother me much because I had never had my own bed (that wouldn't happen until my freshman year in college), and sleeping in the apartment's most open space gave me the impression I had a room of my own or at the very least a place to breathe, to day-dream, and to cry in complete privacy when I remembered my mother. When I couldn't sleep, I would simply pull a chair into the tiny kitchen and read under its dim light, the only light that didn't bother Abuelo, who always kept his bedroom door ajar in order to keep track of our movements. In any case, I didn't dare ask the obvious questions: Where would she sleep? Would I have to give up my couch?

The plan wasn't discussed with me, but I picked up snippets of conversation over time. Since I was a reader, I became invisible behind a book, and somehow my grandparents thought I also became deaf, because they would speak frankly in front of me about subjects that would make them hush whenever anyone else walked in.

"She won't be expensive," Abuelo assured Abuela, who nodded in agreement. The long pause that followed made me wonder where their minds had drifted. Perhaps to the convenience of the situation: that a young woman from México would be easy to control, perhaps even easy to take advantage of.

I couldn't imagine what young woman would accept such a position, traveling so far away just to live with a family of farm-workers in a compact unit of the Southern California housing projects. I had seen a few Mexican films that touched on the subject of poor young women who left their small villages for an opportunity to thrive, but in all cases, they went to live in big city apartments or suburban homes owned by lawyers, doctors, or businessmen. But in the film narratives, the poor young women didn't have to leave the country. It dawned on me then why this was an especially important detail: the young woman we would be bringing back would be undocumented, making her even more vulnerable.

Locating a coyote who could smuggle a young woman across was a relatively easy search. We lived a few hours from the border. Over the years, reports traveled through the streets about so-and-so's cousin or so-and-so's nephew arriving safely, and the community took note of the coyote's reputation and his contact information to pass along in the most clandestine of referrals. Crossing her over was not the problem. Finding her—that was the sticking point. Or so I thought.

Every summer, my grandparents traveled to Michoacán, Abuelo behind the wheel of his truck, annoyed and exasperated after the first day on the road. I had made the trip a few times before, so I knew the code of conduct in the camper. Basically, become invisible, inaudible—something I was very good at around Abuelo, who snapped at the smallest things. He held a particular dislike for my brother, who hadn't learned to be silent. Given a choice, Alex would not have joined us on that trip, but he didn't have a choice. Not anymore. As soon as our father moved us into our grandparents' domain, we were expected to surrender completely. So there we were the following July, lying down among the piles of secondhand clothing our grandparents took back to their homeland. Whether they sold it or gave it away I never found out.

The two-day drive was utterly boring. The camper didn't have much in terms of windows, but in reality there wasn't much to see. When we passed by some little town, it looked exactly like the one before with the same buildings and people who wore the same coats and dresses as the citizens of the town just before it. My brother, mad that he had been dragged on this journey, lost himself in sleep since it was too noisy in the back to even hold a conversation. I had withdrawn into a quiet depression after my mother died, so I had no problem letting go of any emotion or expectation, though I did feel bad for my brother, who was more active and spirited. The two-day trip in that tomb must have driven him crazy. I tried not to dwell on the helplessness of the situation because I had no power. Neither of us did. This was our new life without our mother: getting sucked into the whims of our very complicated Abuelo.

When we finally made it to Michoacán, I was surprised when we stopped in a small mountain village just before Zacapu, my family's hometown. When Abuelo lifted the camper door, the light spilled in and the air was invigorating. I knew right away where we had arrived—El Pueblito, where our distant Purépecha relatives, the cheesemakers, lived. Before we left Zacapu to migrate to California, we made frequent visits here to pick up cheese and to drop off the gallons of spoiled milk. Our El Pueblito relatives were as small and dark as Abuela, they had a peculiar way of shaking hands, and they walked on the mountain paths on bare feet. The village was a series of wooden shacks with chickens pecking about and exposed kitchens where our relatives knelt on the ground over their stone metates to shape the curdled milk into beautiful wheels of cheese. The acidic smell in the air was overwhelming. On weekends, the cheesemakers traveled to Zacapu to sell their product at the market or on the plaza, but my city relatives came up by bus for the family discount.

After the initial handshaking and samplings of cheese, Abuelo made it clear that my brother and I had to wander about so that the adults could talk. So we did. We kicked at the weeds near the walls made with boulders and pelted rocks at each other. Later, I figured out that this was the moment when a young woman had been chosen to make that long journey back to the U.S. with us. The efficiency of the agreement didn't surprise me, not with Abuelo's temperament. He was an impatient man, and anyone who dealt with him had to move just as quickly, just as impulsively.

We left El Pueblito and showed up, wheels of cheese in hand, at Abuelo's sister's house in the heart of Zacapu. Tía Sara lived in a multiunit complex with a courtyard hidden from street view by a heavy wooden door that was kept bolted shut. I had no idea we would be back to El Pueblito near the end of our visit to pick up Adelina, a terrified young woman only a few years older than I, so during the next few days, my brother and I walked in and out of Tía Sara's house in ignorant bliss, visiting relatives from our mother's side of the family and making frequent trips to the plaza, where we spent our allowance on gelatin cups and used magazines. Despite that fortress of an entrance that had to be opened by skeleton key, we had freedoms here that we didn't have in the U.S., where Abuelo kept a strict seven o'clock curfew, which didn't really matter much because there was nowhere to go within walking distance. There, we wasted our evenings glued to the television. Back in our homeland, we felt energized by the activity on the plaza, the constant wave of voices. People spilled out of the church and crowded around the women roasting nuts or pumpkin seeds on large metal discs. Musicians competed against the politicians speaking through ear-piercing sound systems. Groups of teenagers teased each other with flirtatious dares, and the younger kids chased stray dogs out to the street. This was familiar territory. What we had given up. Yet we convinced ourselves, perhaps because we could not choose to return, that we were better off in the north, that opportunities awaited us that none of these people swirling about the plaza could even imagine. At one point, as we walked by a young man our age who was setting up his shoe shine kit on the steps of the church courtyard, my brother turned to me and said, "That would've been us if we had stayed."

I was surprised to hear that insight coming from my younger brother. I was even more startled by the fact that I agreed with him, that somehow we had found a silver lining to the loss of our homeland and the loss of our mother. Sacrifice. That was the word Abuela used often. Sacrifice is what it took to achieve a reward. I imagined that's how my family justified our migration north. I imagined that's what Adelina had been told also when she agreed to join us. Any suffering would be worth it in the end.

At night, Alex and I snuggled into our individual beds and watched television programming in Spanish, something we had access to in the U.S. but didn't care for. We were too busy assimilating with MTV and thirty-minute sitcoms about silly white people who got a laugh for stubbing a toe. We didn't say much to each other because there was nothing to share. The only time we broached anything close to a serious conversation was when we wondered why Tía Sara lived like a wealthy Mexican with a bountiful kitchen and two servant girls who washed the bedsheets every other day while we lived in the U.S. as poor people.

"She probably married money," I concluded.

Whatever the reason, the courtyard was filled with wonder—a fig tree that exploded with fruit every morning, a flock of cooing doves that shed downy feathers into the air, and a Doberman pinscher with its tail cut off that answered to the name of Hitler. Tía Sara seemed embarrassed to tell us this, but she had no choice. Calling out its name was the only way to quiet the animal.

"My youngest named him that," she explained. "And the name stuck. It's vulgar, I know, but what can we do?"

Hitler was a gentle animal most of the time, but his bark was frightening. And because I reminded him of his young owner (or so my aunt said), it gravitated toward me especially. If I stood or sat down, the dog would press its lean but sturdy body against my legs, threatening to knock me off balance.

A week into our visit, Alex and I had grown so accustomed to our newfound perks and privileges that it was with great disappointment that we received the news from Abuela that we were headed back to California. "So gather your things," she said. Alex and I stuffed our duffle bags with clothes and the small collection of knickknacks we had accumulated on our daily trips to the plaza. Another two-day journey was upon us.

A few hours later, Abuelo instructed us to hop inside the camper. When I picked up my duffle bag, he yelled out, "Leave that there, stupid. We're going to run some errands first."

My heart sank. That glimpse of nastiness was just a taste of the company we were going to keep all the way back home. An hour later, as we pulled into El Pueblito, Abuelo told us to stay put inside the camper. Minutes later, the camper door opened and we sat there speechless and confused as a frightened young woman climbed in with us.

"That's Adelina," Abuelo said. "Your cousin. She's going to take care of you." And then the camper door slammed shut.

The whole episode was something out of a kidnapping plot. The visit was no longer than a few minutes, and the young woman had climbed on board without even a purse, just the clothes on her back—a pink hand-knitted sweater, a plain blue skirt, and white knee-high socks with holes in them. As Abuelo drove back to Zacapu, the young woman began to hyperventilate. Alex and I simply watched, uncertain about what to do.

"You have a cut there," Alex pointed out to her, finally breaking the awkward silence.

We all looked down at her hand. Her fingernail was bleeding. I knew that kind of damage—evidence of a desperate grip in a hard-fought battle that had just been lost.

That rest of the afternoon was surreal. Abuelo employed a soft, almost tender manner when speaking to Adelina. Unsettling at first, it eventually angered me because I knew this act was short-lived, that by the time we arrived back in California he would resort back to his brutish ways, his gruffness matching his bristly mustache.

We stopped at the mercado, which puzzled me because I didn't think there was any need for grocery shopping, but then we beelined it to the back of the building, where the merchants sold cheap clothing. Since Adelina climbed into the truck without a suitcase, this would have to do for the moment. Abuela coaxed her into choosing a blouse, stockings, and underwear, which was stuffed into a cone made from newspaper. Even during this intimate selection, she remained stoic, in shock, so I became embarrassed for her at the indignity of having to pick her panty colors in front of all of us.

"Would you like an ice cream?" Abuelo said in his fake gentle voice.

Adelina nodded, a glimmer of excitement on her face, and this is when I realized how young she actually was. She picked a tamarind ice cream bar and devoured it, as if this was the last taste of anything she was going to have of her homeland. I remembered that sense of impending separation when I had to climb a bus with my family to travel north to the border three years before. I wanted to hold on to something—a final touch, a final taste, a last-chance encounter that I could brand into my brain as the parting gift from my beloved hometown.

As we sat in silence consuming our treats, I finally wondered about Adelina, how her name sounded eerily similar to my mother's—Avelina—how her presence here seemed more like a penance than a reward. Had she done something to offend her family, who so willingly offered her up for this task of being a nanny to two orphans living in California? Had she been told earlier that week or was she informed just hours ago? The fact that she had been flung into the truck like an exile suggested other dramatic explanations. Had she sinned against her body? Had she sinned against God? She looked so innocent and so fragile, I couldn't imagine what her story was, and I had a feeling I would never find out.

When we got back to Tía Sara, who kept shaking her head with disapproval, Adelina withdrew even deeper into herself, lowering her head as if in shame. Tía Sara's two servant girls kept eyeing her from a distance as they moved about doing their chores. And then Adelina's situation worsened when Abuelo sat her down in a chair in the middle of the courtyard and cut off her long hair. I became mortified at that public display of humiliation, at the way Tía Sara kept verbalizing her disbelief in what was happening, and how the two servant girls started to giggle, sticking their tongues out at Adelina, who had just aged a few decades after Abuela combed her hair to look exactly like hers—short and with the bangs combed back.

I walked up to Abuela and asked her discreetly, "Why did he cut it off?"

Abuela put her finger to her lips and then pointed with her eyes at a white bucket with Adelina's discarded hair. I bent down to look at it and recognized the infestation of lice. Meanwhile, Adelina simply sat there, expressionless and defeated.

"Why don't you start looking after the boys now," Abuelo told Adelina. She got up from her seat and followed Alex and me to the fig tree at the end of the courtyard. She watched over Alex with disinterest as he climbed up to pick fruit.

Even from a distance, I could hear the grown-ups laughing about the whole situation. I felt I needed to counter that laughter with some compassion, so I started to ask questions.

"You like figs?" I said, offering her one that Alex had pelted down from the tree.

She took it in her hand, but it was more like an act of obedience.

"Have you ever been to California?" I asked and then realized what a stupid thing that was to say. But I was at a loss. I didn't know how to reach out to her. Adelina was a distant cousin, a member of the cheesemakers from El Pueblito. What in the world was she doing getting herself involved with this depressing side of the family? That's the question I really wanted to ask.

But once she realized that I had given up trying to engage her, she spoke up on her own.

"My mother's sick," she said softly. I hardly recognized her voice. All this time, she had been nodding her head or answering my grandparents in monosyllables.

"My mother died," I said, and for the first time since she was thrown into the truck, we made eye contact. Her eyes became watery. I wasn't sure if she was grieving for herself or for me, or for both of us, but I was strangely comforted by the fact that I had someone near me who knew about such pain. Alex had been refusing to talk about our mother's death. Whenever I brought it up, he would stiffen up and say, "Can we change the conversation?" or "I don't want to talk about that." So even though we had suffered the same loss, I felt alone all this time. Suddenly I began to imagine that it wouldn't be so bad to have Adelina among us. Her role was to be our nanny, but there would be a special connection between us, as if she had come into my life to be the older sibling I desperately needed—someone to protect *me* for a change from the awful things of this world, like death, like school bullies, like Abuelo.

"Why don't we go to the plaza together one last time?" Alex called out from the fig tree. And I thought what a great idea it would be to say good-bye to Zacapu together, just the three of us. But when I asked Abuelo for permission, he shot it down.

"She can't leave the house," he said. "If you want to go you go alone, but don't stay out too late. We leave at the crack of dawn."

I wanted to stay behind to keep Adelina company, but my brother wasn't having it and pleaded with me to come along; otherwise he would not be allowed to venture out by himself. And in truth, I wanted to go out as well. So we left Adelina perched on the stone border around the fig tree, and I promised myself that I would bring her something back. When we got to the front door, Tía Sara came over with her skeleton key and unlocked it, as usual. That's when I realized that Adelina was a prisoner. That she was not allowed to come with us because my grandparents were afraid she would escape.

"I don't understand," I said to Alex. "Are we forcing her to go with us?"

"I think so," Alex said.

My good-bye stroll along the plaza was sullied by the thought of Adelina getting smaller and smaller as the hour of our departure neared. And suddenly I began to question whether I really wanted to return. What if I fled that very moment and hid away with my mother's relatives? They were church people, kind of boring and not very expressive, but they weren't mean or abusive like Abuelo. I thought about proposing the idea to Alex, but I didn't dare. Even then I knew what a stupid risk it was, and what dire consequences awaited us after Abuelo claimed us back.

Before returning to Tía Sara's, I bought Adelina a set of barrettes. It seemed like an insensitive gift, but Abuela had pinned Adelina's hair back with those old lady bobby pins that had aged her. We knocked on Tía Sara's door and heard her unlocking like a warden.

"Did you have a nice time?" she asked, and I wanted to spit on her. Surely she could see what a cruel thing was taking place right in her own house, and though she kept muttering her disapproval, she was going to do nothing to stop her stubborn older brother.

As the grown-ups prepared the final meal in the kitchen, their mood was celebratory. Laughter and music lit up the small room while just a few feet away Adelina sulked in a chair. I walked up to her with my gift.

"I brought you these," I said, holding up the barrettes. But instead of taking them, she took hold of my wrist.

"You have to help me," she said. Her eyes were burning with anxiety.

"Help you how?" I said. Though I knew exactly what she was asking.

Adelina pulled me so close to her that for a moment I thought she was going to kiss me, but I didn't resist. And just as I was about to anticipate our faces coming together, she froze, her eyes locked directly with mine.

A flash of recognition passed between us, and in that instant I began to suspect why she had been cast out of her family, her village, why she was being punished like this. There it was, that thing inside of me that made me different, an aberration in the eyes of family and an insult to God. Or maybe that was wishful thinking, me projecting my own fears upon this young woman who was opening her soul to me, trusting me while she was at her most vulnerable. In any case, I responded in kind, revealing my true self, letting her in on this secret that I wanted someone else to recognize without ridicule or disgust.

Suddenly I became even more frightened. What if I denied her? Would she betray me? Would she confirm for Abuelo what he was probably suspecting all along, and would he then cast me out of this family as well, maybe drop me off in El Pueblito on our way out because that would be an apt punishment for me—a life of labor in a rural village that would butch me up, me, this sissy of a boy who was all sentimentality and sensitivity, not much of a man-to-be at all.

"Will you help me?" This time she appealed to me with a kindness in her voice that convinced me she was intending no malice. So I resolved to help her.

I would be lying if I didn't admit that I was experiencing a thrill plotting Adelina's flight. But it was a relatively easy plan to come up with and execute. I wandered into the kitchen the way young people sometimes do, curious about the goings-on with the grown-ups, until one of them shooed the underage visitor away from the off-colored jokes and big people talk. I was able to sneak in and out without notice, but not before pinching Tía Sara's skeleton key, which she kept in plain sight and which remained forgotten until it was needed.

Adelina was already waiting in the shadows. The music was playing loud enough that it would drown out the creaking of the door opening. But just as we started to fiddle with the lock in the dark, Hitler came barking. Adelina cowered in the corner and whimpered in fear.

"It's okay, it's okay," I said.

I called the dog over. It recognized me and started to press against my legs to show its affection. This time I didn't push it away. This time I needed to keep the animal tame. I continued to jiggle the key in the lock until it finally clicked open. A puff of fresh air blew in from the street. I looked at Adelina, who looked incredulous that we had gone this far. She hesitated.

"What's the matter?" I said. Suddenly I worried that this pause in the plan was going to cost us. I felt the heat of Abuelo's belt across my ass.

Even in the shadow, I saw the glossy glare of Adelina's eyes. She had been moved by my actions. And just as easily, my own eyes began to water. The moment seemed inappropriately melo-dramatic, maybe even unconvincing, because we had just met a few hours ago and here we were weeping at our parting. But we were both in states of distress—I had lost my loved one and she had been rejected by hers. We were both abandoned and alone, and possibly, just maybe, or so I wanted to believe, we were both struggling with our sexual identities. She was my sister in that mo-ment and I was her brother, and we had just found each other but now we were saying good-bye. And for a moment, I thought about going with her, about escaping into the night in order to live my own life, not the one that was being dictated by family. I pictured taking her hand and stepping through the threshold right after her, shutting the door behind us and disappearing into who knows what wondrous freedoms. But before I had a chance to take this moment of fantasy any further, Adelina flew out like the caged dove that she was, her pink sweater suddenly bright and magical. I watched her turn the corner and I imagined her slipping into a whole new dimension where she would remain safe—untouched and unharmed—for the rest of her days.

Solemnly I closed the door to Adelina's courageous world and shut myself inside my own. The next day, the grown-ups would wonder how Adelina had escaped, and none of their speculations would come close to the truth; I would keep the secret hidden in my heart until most of them had passed away, long after her name had sunk into silence. And eventually, the day would come when I too would flee. But not that night. I couldn't walk out, not just yet, not with my little brother, Alex, to look after. I turned the lock and slipped back inside my family's suffocating reverie.

CANTO

In the summer of 1984, two years after the death of my mother, my aunt decided to make good on a promise: to ensure that my brother and I completed one of the mandated holy sacraments: our first communion.

At fourteen, I was considered a latecomer. My brother at twelve, also. Usually, children in México took their first communion before the age of ten. There was no proper explanation for why our family had neglected this Catholic duty, so my aunt simply walked into the church in Mexicali to seek advice from the priest. The priest shook his head and looked down at us, two poor orphans, with grave pity and gave my aunt the name of a catechism teacher, a *catequista*, who would be more than happy to offer us a crash course. "She's a widow, you know," the priest informed us, and I wasn't sure if he meant that not having a husband allotted her the time for such charity or if her widowhood made her more sympathetic to our needs.

That same afternoon, we walked over to la catequista's house. She too listened patiently and kept glancing at us as my aunt tried to justify why we had to compress a yearlong instruction into one summer: we were visiting from the U.S., this was the only chance we had before we were returned to our nonpracticing Catholic grandparents, we were in need of salvation. La catequista didn't react, as if she had seen this situation many times before. About the only thing that surprised her was when my aunt insisted that my brother and I not sit on the couch but on the floor because we were dirty. La catequista was flustered at first but let it go. It was as if she understood my aunt's awkwardness at stepping into a house that was clearly a rich lady's home. None of us were used to entering such spaces with porcelain knickknacks and doilies so white they settled on the furniture like miraculous snowflakes that would never melt.

I took an immediate liking to la catequista. She was the most beautiful lady I had come across. She was impeccably coiffed, her dress looked freshly pressed, and she had the most delicate hands I had ever seen on a woman, my mother included. La catequista's were the hands of a woman who wasn't used to hard labor, who probably had a maid to do the household chores, and I didn't hold any of these things against her because I was smitten. And I wanted her to like me back just as quickly.

As usual, my brother and I were simply passive observers to the decisions of the grown-ups. We left la catequista's house, and on the way home, my aunt explained to us the summer's drill: Three days a week for the next month, we would come here for lessons. The rest of those days, we would have to memorize the teachings in the catechism, the Catholic manual of questions, answers, and prayers. The expectation didn't frighten me, though my brother was sure from the get-go that this was going to ruin our summer fun.

"I don't mind," I said to him.

"Of course, you don't," my brother said. "*You're* no fun." He then scampered off to join the rest of the boys in a game of soccer on the street.

Since there was absolutely nothing of an athlete but plenty of nerd in me, I took to the tiny catechism book with enthusiasm. Each day, I spent hours copying the pages into a notebook because we had borrowed the catechism from a neighbor. My aunt said she didn't have money to spend on a book we would use for only one month, but the truth was she didn't have any money at all, so I didn't question the odd request to rewrite the entire book so that I could return the catechism to its rightful owner. While I copied, I underlined words I didn't know. In the afternoons, I stood next to my aunt as she unpinned the clothes from the line and explained these words I had never heard before. At bedtime, I murmured the prayers to myself, determined to please my beloved catequista.

During this time, there was another event unfolding in the background. I caught snippets of information on the neighbor's radio or on the news reports on Mexican TV—the Olympics were taking place in Los Angeles. LA was only a few hours away, but it might as well have been another planet since most people we knew could not cross the border. And those who could, like my father or my aunt, had no reason to venture that far north. They never traveled past the agricultural fields of the Coachella Valley, where they worked most of the year as farmworkers.

The subject of the Olympics did, however, infiltrate the conversation of one of our weekly cookouts on the back porch. My aunt kept bringing out fresh meat from the fridge and my uncle stood over the grill. Other grown-ups were already digging in while the younger kids ran around and had to be snagged by the shirt collars to force them to eat. The radio was on, and the announcer suddenly chimed in to report that México, just like every Olympic year, sucked.

"Well, that was unnecessary," one of the grown-ups said.

"But it's true," my aunt said. "And it's because our government won't give these kids proper training. The United States claims every medal and makes México look like it showed up by accident." She leaned forward to take a bite of her taco in order to avoid spilling grease on her blouse.

"Maybe we should compete in what we excel in," my uncle, her husband, said, in a rare show of courage to speak up. "Like taco eating." He pointed at my aunt with the tongs.

I thought his statement was kind of funny, but the delivery was too slow on the uptake, so it didn't pick up any traction and no one laughed. Also, my aunt just glared at him, chewing her food with an exaggerated movement that served as a warning.

The Olympic Games, just like LA, just like la catequista's house, were foreign territories to us. Of course we knew what they were, but none of us took much interest, not even in soccer or boxing, which were sports many of our family members liked to follow on TV. Our history teacher in high school was excited to brag that he knew the man who was choreographing the marching bands for the opening ceremony. My fellow ninth graders were not readily impressed by that, and I didn't know how to react to it either. I suppose that at that age we were all simply preoccupied with our individual adolescent worlds.

My particular world was still grief-stricken from the loss of my mother. And the loss of my father, who had decided to remarry and move out of my grandparents' house while my brother and I were in school. Staying with my aunt and my five cousins over the summer was my grandparents' way of giving us some space, though I knew it was they who wanted their cramped two-bedroom apartment back. Whatever the reason, studying the catechism seemed like a small price to pay in order to spend the summer at my aunt's big house with a large back porch and its expansive view of the boulevard that stretched so far out it shrank the huge cargo trucks down to the size of bugs.

The other reason my brother and I were there, I suspected, was to mend a bridge with our father. I had not forgiven him for leaving us behind with our grandparents. One afternoon, I walked into my aunt's house after sitting on the back porch, bored of leafing through the catechism in my notebook, and was surprised to see my father sitting in the living room. The TV was on, and like every other station, the Olympic Games were showing—swimming or some other water sport. No one was really watching, but it was a habit to keep the TV playing, the white noise necessary to muffle the constant chaos of people walking in and out at all times of the day.

My body froze when I saw him sitting on the couch with a beer in his hand. He smiled and took a sip from the bottle.

"You were outside reading?" he asked.

"Yes," I stuttered.

My two uncles were also seated in the living room, so I felt I had invaded some exclusive masculine space. It certainly stopped me from displaying any emotion, like crying because I was so happy to see my father, or yelling because I was so upset he had abandoned me. Instead, I kept walking right through the living room and to the kitchen as if that had been my intention all along.

I don't remember if my little brother had a difficult time with our father's presence. Alex seemed more interested in the streets. I couldn't get him to sit still and read the catechism notebook, so my aunt forced one of her sons—my brother's sidekick in all things mischief—to simmer down once in a while to study.

My father, always a popular center of attention, wandered about the place, joking and telling stories, which made it more challenging to justify my resentment toward him. Just when I thought I could edge my feelings toward forgiveness, something came along to remind me of how much he had failed us. Like the time my aunt sat with me on the porch behind the house to tell me about deodorant.

"Smell this," she directed me, holding up one of my own dirty shirts.

"It smells," I said.

"Those are your armpits," she said. She explained it so gently but it still felt like a type of shaming, as if I should have been spared this embarrassing exchange if only my father had told me about the need for deodorant in the first place.

Puberty was a tougher subject to navigate, so my aunt left it up to her husband, that shy man whom I rarely heard speak except to reprimand one of his boys for doing this or not doing the other. We had our chat on the bench one afternoon, and I knew it was as devastating to him as it was to me.

"You're in a stage of your life when your body changes. And has urges," he said as flatly as if he were giving me directions to the post office.

I stared out at the boulevard and slipped into tune-out mode. My neck was flushed and so was his as he stumbled his way into a less-colorful version of the birds and the bees that my older cousins had been regaling us with those evenings at the clubhouse—a makeshift "boys only" room built on top of my aunt's house. I didn't venture there often, only when my female cousins wanted to have some "girls only" time of their own, in which case I had no choice but to sit and listen to the boys' dirty jokes and idiotic stories with implausible erotic plot lines that always seemed to end with a scene involving a naked priest or a horny nun. And when they arrived at the masturbation testimonials, I shook my head and said, "That's wrong."

All heads turned to me. "What?" one of my cousins said.

"It's wrong to touch yourself," I said. "God is watching."

A few of them stifled a laugh. My oldest cousin, the ringleader, decided to take over. "And you've never touched yourself?"

"No," I said in earnest. "It would offend God."

A quiet descended on the group, which I now know was more like pity. I would have become the object of relentless ridicule if my cousin, in an unusual display of mercy, hadn't intervened. "That's alright," he told the group. "He's an innocent. Stupidly so, but there's no reason to hold that against him."

The group proceeded with their vulgarities, pretending I wasn't in the room.

If I could have excused my poor uncle from this uncomfortable duty, I would have. But I respected his effort, so I let him go on a little longer, telling me about men and women and this mysterious physical thing that happened, which could result in an unwanted pregnancy and then what a fine mess we would all be in.

My catechism was a little more all-inclusive in exploring that territory. One of the questions simply asked: *What are the three enemies of the soul?* The answer: *The devil, the world, and the flesh.* My aunt extrapolated. They were enemies because they were temptations: the devil tempted me into wrongdoings, into crimes against God; the world tempted me with the love of money, of material things, the trappings of power and position and wealth; the flesh—and I was surprised my aunt spat this one out so easily—meant the temptation of sex with those women of ill repute.

It was an odd answer, but I understood that in some strange way she was actually talking about my future stepmother. I suspected this because anytime the subject came up, she was quick to criticize the fact that Amelia wore makeup, that she bought those expensive bras with girdles attached, that she dyed her hair blonde. Amelia was a list of offenses against feminine decency, perhaps even obscene. It made me feel sorry for her until I remembered that I faulted her too for taking my father away from me.

After the whole enemies of man explanation, I asked my aunt, quite innocently, "So what are the enemies of women?"

She answered without skipping a beat. "Just one: man."

At this point in the rambling narrative of my poor uncle's beleaguered sex education course, he was approaching the subject of masturbation, which made his mouth so dry he started to cough. I thought it would be wise to let him off the hook.

"Thank you, uncle," I said. "I know all that already."

He looked at me with relief. "Oh, well that's good," he said. "Though I hope you're not getting all of your information from the boys at the clubhouse."

"It's all in here," I said, and I lifted my catechism notebook to show him.

"Good," he said. He rose from the bench and looked out at the boulevard. "Looks like rain this afternoon. Let me go roll the windows up in the truck." And with that, he left, and I wondered what strange method he was using to predict the weather since there was nothing beyond the boulevard but clear sky.

Instruction day. I rose early, showered, and pressed into my armpits a few extra layers of deodorant so that I could sit on la catequista's couch, though by the time we reached her house, we were drenched in sweat. My brother would only come along if his sidekick, our cousin, was there to keep him company, which everyone agreed to just because nothing else seemed to motivate him.

"My, look at you all. It's so hot; why didn't you take the bus?" la catequista asked.

"We can't afford the bus fare," my cousin answered, which seemed to distraught la catequista. I made a note to tell my aunt that he had done this.

We drank our glasses of water and prepared for the lessons, but first la catequista had to chase her son out of the room. He was seated in front of the TV watching the Olympics.

"Raymundo, my love," la catequista said, sweetly. "Can you please watch the TV in the back room?"

"Yes, mamita," Raymundo said. He turned the TV off and came over to give la catequista a kiss on the cheek before exiting the living room.

The heat I felt was coming from my brother and my cousin, who I was certain were going to mock this public display of affection all the way home. "*Yes, mamita*, how old is this fucking faggot?" one of them would say to the other, while I lagged behind.

As for me, I felt a bit jealous. This Raymundo didn't look very smart. He was dressed in better clothes, but that was because his mother dressed him. And maybe my mind was playing tricks on me, but I could have sworn he smelled, that rank armpit smell that was no longer a part of who I was. I discreetly sniffed myself just in case. No, I swore on my catechism notebook that it was Raymundo.

It didn't matter that my brother and my cousin threw dagger eyes at me each time I got the questions right or when I recited a prayer so flawlessly it brought great joy to la catequista—I was doing this for *her*, not for them or even for me. I was dazzling her with my memorization skills because she had become so special to me. I adored the way her eyes sparkled when I made it all the way through the Apostles' Creed, the way she clasped her hands to her chest and said, "Amén," and the way that word floated out of her pretty lips, a blessing that hovered over me like a guardian angel. Tearing myself away from la catequista after the hour's lesson was such a disappointment for me. And such a delight for my brother. We left, and, predictably, my cousin and brother couldn't stop bad-mouthing Raymundo. And for once, their stupid remarks made me smile.

When we arrived at the neighborhood, there was a flurry of activity on the street. Don Pepe had just parked his candy cart in front of my aunt's house, and the kids buzzed around it like bees. My cousin ran inside to ask his mother for money, but my brother stayed behind. Suddenly he turned to me for sympathy because I was the only other person who understood at that moment that we had no one to hear our pleas for money.

I was about to offer some words of comfort when my cousin ran out of the house yelling, "Hey, Alex, your father's here!"

That changed everything for Alex, who ran into the house. Perhaps it was the contagious excitement, or the many tempting items dangling from Don Pepe's candy cart, that made me set all modesty aside and also run into the house. I crossed paths with my brother, who was already on his way out. But as soon as I saw my father, I changed my mind.

"You need some money too, son?" he asked.

Something boiled inside of me. *Son?* He had called me his son. But when my brother walked in waving his candy in my face, my anger subsided.

"Well, maybe I want one of those," I said, pointing at the sweet and spicy wheels that unroll into foot-long strings of tamarind pulp.

My father walked out to the candy cart, and I hated myself for letting my sweet tooth betray me. I didn't like this age where I could be bribed and bought with candy. When my father walked back in, he held out an entire pack with six wheels linked together. I was not sure what kind of response he expected, but what I gave him made his face darken.

"What are you doing?" I yelled. "I just wanted one! Why are you embarrassing me like this? Why are you showing off to everyone when you're not even my father anymore? Why don't you just go away and leave me alone!"

I left him standing in the middle of the living room with the candy, and I ran out of the house to hide out on my bench. A few minutes later, my aunt came out to sit beside me.

"That wasn't very kind," she said. "You hurt your father's feelings."

I started crying.

"You're old enough to understand that he has to live his own life," she said. "Your mother passed away and he needs a woman. And believe me, you don't want a woman of ill repute to be your mother. So it's better this way. You have your grandmother to take care of you. And you have me and your other aunts, although, don't put too much faith on *them* since they're only related by marriage."

I was still crying, but I also wanted to laugh at the ridiculous logic of grown-ups and their flexible values. They behaved in complete contradiction to the teachings of the catechism that laid things out clearly and openly: this was right, that was wrong, you did this, you didn't do that. Maybe I wasn't the one who needed the crash course. And that's when the idea finally took root in my mind. It had been planted there from the beginning, but I wasn't nurturing it the way I really wanted to. The answer was indeed la catequista. "She's a widow, you know," the priest had told us. Which meant she had to be lonely and lonelier still if all she had was that stinky armpits Raymundo to keep her company. I resolved then and there to ask la catequista to adopt me.

"I'm okay now," I said to my aunt, who seemed surprised the crying just stopped. I got up and walked into the house to accept those candy wheels from my father because this was the last time I was going to see him.

My heart fluttered with so much anticipation all night that it was difficult to fall asleep. I recited my prayers, my memorized questions and answers, spinning them in my brain until I was dizzy and eventually drowsy. The next morning, I woke myself up singing. Nothing to be embarrassed about except that I didn't sleep alone. Since there wasn't much space to go around, we slept five to a room. My spot was on the floor, between two other bodies.

"Someone's happy," my cousin said.

"Did I wake you?" I asked.

"You woke us all up," my brother said from the top bunk bed.

"What did it sound like?" I asked.

"I don't know. It sounded like a church song."

A canto, a hymn—the confirmation I needed that I was doing the right thing today.

"What were you dreaming about?" my cousin asked.

I wasn't sure what I was dreaming about, but when I didn't answer, no one cared enough to pursue it and everyone went back to sleep. I got up, folded my blanket, for the last time, I was sure of it, and put together a backpack with a small bundle of things I didn't want to leave behind—my favorite shirt, extra underwear, a picture of my mother I carried with me when I traveled, a rosary I took from my grandmother's room because it reminded me of the novena we prayed after my mother's burial.

That afternoon, I couldn't get to la catequista's house soon enough. I had it all planned out. As soon as lessons were done, I would let my brother and cousin walk out ahead of me and I would stay behind to make my proposition.

But during our lesson I was distracted, daydreaming about how I was going to be having breakfast at the table every morning, about what my new bedroom was going to be like. I stared at a picture of la catequita's dead husband on the lamp table as if I wanted some telepathic communication and to get some words of advice about what to do to make his widow happy. I was looking around the room so often that la catequista paused at one point to ask me if I was alright. This startled me. My brother and cousin glanced at each other, storing the mishap for later use.

"Let's continue," la catequista said. "Alex, name the seven capital sins. Rigoberto, name the seven virtues."

The slight annoyance in her voice unsettled me. I was setting the wrong tone for the occasion. My brother dragged the list out of his memory banks with his cheerleader at his side. But when my turn came, the seven virtues completely flew out of my head. I stared blankly at la catequista.

"Rigoberto, I'm surprised at you today," she said. My brother mocked me by shaking his head in disapproval. I found it difficult to swallow.

As we finished the lesson, Raymundo couldn't wait to turn on the TV to watch the Olympics. When my cousin asked for a soda, la catequista directed him to the fridge and my brother joined him in the caper. La catequista just breathed in deeply as if she had no choice but to accept the ways of the adolescent boys around her.

"Señora," I managed to say. Though I wasn't sure what was going to come next. Should I apologize for being such a terrible student or should I go ahead and tell her that I wanted her to adopt me, to take me away from that family that only knew how to love me with candy and cookouts and vulgar stories that made me feel disrespectful toward God?

"What is it, Rigoberto? Do you have something to tell me?"

"I—" The words felt heavy in my mouth. *Say it, say it, say it, you idiot!* a voice inside me demanded. But that lingering doubt that I had ignored before now began to make my entire body tremble. Yet I had to know. I really had to know whether she would take to the idea of adopting me or laugh me right out of her home. But when I finally said it, it came out in a whisper, a sound too faint for her to hear.

La catequista came closer. "What did you say? I didn't hear you. Raymundo, my love, please turn the television down!"

But Raymundo of the stinky armpits didn't turn the television down. Instead, he yelled back: "Mami, mami, look, look, we're going to win a gold medal! We're going to win a gold medal!"

Everyone turned to the TV. And sure enough, there was excitement in the announcer's voice because Ernesto Canto was most certainly going to place in the men's 20 km race walk.

"Canto, Canto, Canto," the TV announcer began to chant. My brother and cousin closed in on the TV set with Raymundo, who was already chanting along with the TV, "Canto, Canto, Canto."

"Too exciting!" la catequista said, and she placed her delicate hand on my shoulder to hold herself still because she was shaking. And as Ernesto Canto reached the finish line, a joy overcame la catequista. She beamed, and I could feel that warmth press against me when she threw her arms around me in exhilaration. I breathed in her perfume and smiled. Oh my God, this was my heaven.

"México, México, México," the announcer changed his chant, and so did the boys in the living room.

I didn't know what was going to consume me first, the fact that poor little México was going to win its gold medal, or that I finally got what I had been waiting for—an affectionate touch from someone in the room who thought that it mattered that I too was in the room. It was a small thing, that hug, but in that moment, it was a giant triumph, like that gold medal, worth clinging to because deep down inside we all knew there would be very few others to come.

TAKE A GUESS

The highlight of living in Southern California's Coachella Valley and the so-called date capital of the world was attending the Riverside County Fair and National Date Festival on Arabia Street. The weeklong event took place in the month of February, and when we could afford it, the entire family went because it was just down the street from the low-income housing project we called home.

One year, one of my cousins was a member of the high school's Future Farmers of America and so this was the big good-bye to the sheep he had been feeding and caring for all year. The fair offered more than a petting zoo; it was where professional farmers came to buy and sell livestock. The Future Farmers of America entered their animal charges in a competition and auction, and when my cousin won a blue ribbon, the news was met with little enthusiasm since the sheep was carted off to a real farm and all my cousin got was a college scholarship that his mother predicted he would never use. She was right. Like all her children before him, the future farmer would drop out of school by age sixteen.

But visiting the livestock quarters with my cousin offered me a glimpse of a part of the fair I never thought to see. Usually, we just beelined it to the carnival rides and stayed there until our parents hunted us down. I remember once my brother and I convinced our mother to enter the fun house with us. I think my father egged her on, or even dared her, and she didn't back out. The journey was somewhat fun, with floors shifting and spinning at a slow speed. But the payoff was the exit: the only way out was a slide. My mother was mortified as my father waited at the end of the chute and called out to her: "You're holding up the line, Avelina, let's go!" He was reveling in it.

I wasn't sure how it was going to turn out because I never imagined my mother going down a slide. She was a short but heavyset woman wearing a pretty blouse and a large purse. But she did it, her purse flying up behind her. She was red with embarrassment but she went laughing, and I knew it was a moment I had to hold on to because there were very few times I saw my mother happy. She was constantly ill or upset at my father's drinking, so I always remembered her sad, tearing up because she was in pain or in distress. When I went down the slide after her, I didn't experience the same kind of thrill or joy, but that's because nothing could beat the sight of my mom making her trip down a slide trying to look more ladylike with her legs up in the air, and then giggling at her failure.

The grown-ups didn't participate in the rides and spent most of their carnival time in the exhibition halls that showcased student art or date products. They would sit at the outdoor performance spaces and listen to folk music or watch the annual pageant—a performance of *Aladdin and the Magic Flute*. It was always the same production, and although most of the audience didn't understand English, they picked up on the visual gags, like when the fat lady in a belly dancer's outfit comes out to be weighed on the balance scale and proves to the sultan that she's worth more than a treasure chest of gold.

As I walked with my brother and cousins, I was constantly surprised to bump into people I recognized—other students from my high school. Most of them didn't talk to me at school, but there was something of a contagious good mood among the carnival games and mechanical rides that encouraged many of them to acknowledge me with a nod. It made me feel visible and it felt great. I wasn't one of the popular kids. I wasn't one of the popular kids at home either. I was the quiet one who preferred to read a book and hide in the back of the room. It was a way of achieving safety. I had seen how the "different" kids were bullied and ostracized, and I didn't want to be one of them.

However, many of my schoolmates were showing up at the fairgrounds with their dates, so I made it a point to walk around with my cousin Vero because I could pass her off as my girlfriend or something. She didn't care. She just thought it was wise to travel as a pair because no one wanted to ride alone. I had yet to come out of the closet, so this arrangement was perfect. Suddenly the other guys nodded at me in approval. The girls smiled. All of us were complicit in the games couples play to show the rest of the crowd we were spoken for, desired, maybe even mature.

The only time this false impression backfired was when I ran into my other single acquaintances, the ones who were more like me—nerdy outsiders years away from a first kiss. I tried to give them the acknowledging nod, but they refused to nod back. I had betrayed them. And I knew then what a stupid thing I had done because come Monday morning, I would be back in the outsider pool, except that I had just alienated its members, the ones who sat in the back of the room with me. Though we never spoke to each other, we felt somehow protected in our huddle. A chill ran down my spine, but I kept on, making believe I was as confident as those who had always been cocky about their place among those who were there to be seen by those who were not.

"Hey, Vero," I said to my cousin. "Can I get you a soda?"

"Yeah, I'm thirsty," she said.

I let her wait in line to the Music Express. Since she didn't have any pockets, I carried her cash with me, so I was able to fool anyone who might just happen to take notice or even care that I was buying two drinks with my own cash. When I returned, I saw two girls from my journalism class, chatting it up in the same line.

"Hey, Rigo," one of them said. "Are those sodas for us?"

I blushed and pointed at Vero, who looked back with disinterest.

"Let me guess," the other said. "Your girlfriend? She go to our school?"

"She goes to CV High," I said, aware that I had chosen to answer the second question only.

"Ooh, kissy kissy!" said the first. I was so rattled from the teasing, I simply walked away.

"Don't let her crush you too hard," one called out. My face felt warm. That's why the Music Express was so popular with couples. The train spun around at such high speed that it pushed the bodies in the car even closer together.

I handed Vero her soda. "Let me guess," she said. "Those girls go to your school?"

I sucked at the straw to my drink. When we were finally on board the train, I was so self-conscious about the two girls staring at us from the sidelines as they waited for our turn to end that I tried to keep Vero's body off me, which was impossible. After a few times around, I saw the girls from the journalism class pointing at how silly I looked with my shoulder grinding into Vero and Vero glaring at me. By the time the ride started to slow to a stop, Vero was so pissed off that she said, "I'm going to look for the others."

"Wait, aren't we getting on the Zipper?"

Vero rolled her eyes. "Why don't you ask one of your dumb girlfriends over there?" She pointed at the girls from the journalism class, and they covered their mouths to hide their laughter. And with that, Vero took off, leaving me standing there with my hands in my pockets.

"You can always ride between us," one of the girls called out, while the other blew a kiss. I was such an easy victim for this kind

Take a Guess

of teasing, even from my cousins at home. It seemed as if everyone knew I was hiding something that needed to be coaxed out into the open. What that was, I wasn't sure. That I was a virgin? That I was gay? I suppose it didn't matter. Either one of those secrets made me a target.

Since it wasn't quitting time yet, I decided to walk around on my own for a change, people-watching instead of feeling watched.

Around this time of year, I would hear about the so-called carnies, the white men with tattoos who worked at the carnival. In a mostly Latino community, they were obviously different from us and stood out. I didn't know what to make of them, except that they looked like they were from another planet, especially the red-headed ones with funny facial hair. I wouldn't have given them much notice in my people-watching except that I ran into one of them testing out the Octopus. He climbed into one of the cars and pulled along his squeeze, whom I recognized as one of my neighbors from the housing project.

Patricia was rumored to be a lesbian. She wore track suits, kept her hair very short, and wore no makeup. But that also described my grandmother, so I wasn't sure how this was evidence of anything. Patricia rarely rode the bus with the rest of us, which meant she had her own ride. It didn't dawn on me until much later that most of those days she just never went to school. The few times I did see her, she was looked at with derision. But if that bothered her, she never let on. As the cowardly teenage nerd that I was, I didn't call further attention to myself by talking to her on the bus or at school.

I watched Patricia and her carny for a few Octopus revolutions, and was shocked when she actually made eye contact and smiled. My body froze. I wasn't sure if I should wave or nod or what, so the next time their car shot out of sight, I wandered away and felt like an idiot. Still, I shrugged it off and didn't think about it again until I made my way back to the same spot and saw Patricia sitting next to a large sign that read LET ME GUESS. It was an odd feature among the booths. It was simply a chair next to a long, narrow plank with lettering that announced that for one dollar, this person would guess your age or weight or birthday, and if she guessed incorrectly, you would win a prize.

Wow, I thought. Patricia's like a psychic. No wonder she was weird. I stood for a few moments, expecting people to accept the offer, but no one came around. And then our eyes locked and she waved me over. I panicked. I wanted to run away again or pretend I hadn't seen her, but she gave me that smile again, so I thought it would be rude not to go up to her.

"Hey, Rigoberto," she said. And I thought, oh my God, she *is* a psychic. She guessed my name.

"Hey," I said. "I don't have any money."

"I don't want your money, fool," she said. "I want a favor."

I hesitated. "What?" I finally said.

"Can you man the joint for a few? I have an errand to run."

My eyes widened. The only experience I ever had in manning booths was the cotton candy machine at the journalism club's yearbook fundraiser. Twenty-five cents a pop and all I had to do was drop the sugar and food coloring in the center of the gadget while my coworker spun a cone around the tub to collect the fuzzy threads.

"How does it work?" I asked.

"How does what work?" she said.

"The psychic thing," I said.

Patricia rolled her eyes. "Psychic thing? Oh, you just guess. The point is to get the dollar and give them one of these cheapy toys in the box behind you."

I looked at the carnival games slightly differently. There was one in which people tossed dimes and wherever the dime landed that's what the player got. Over the years, only one person in my family ever took something home: a mirror with a slogan on it that read *Drink Whiskey: It Cures What Ails You.* I once tried the ring toss and wasted my money trying to land the rings on the neck of a bottle. The more rings, the bigger the prize. And then there was that time my father tried to impress us with the BB rifle, aiming it at the conveyor of metal baby chicks. But I did see people win prizes, and girls carrying the stuffed animals around as proof that their boyfriends loved them. Since most of those who played did not win, the joy of playing had to be its own reward. Though that did nothing to assuage my father's bruised ego when he totally bombed at the target gallery.

"Nobody really comes around anyway," Patricia said, "so don't worry about it."

"How do you guess anyway?"

"A snap: if you're going to guess a person's age, just guess younger; if you're going to guess a person's weight, just guess lighter. The point is not to offend anyone. Flatter them and they stupidly give you that dollar."

I looked at the language on the plank. "What if they want you to guess their birth month?"

"That's easy," Patricia said, pulling a notebook out of her pocket. "I pretend I'm writing on this page and show them this."

The scribble was a strange-looking three-letter word that began with *J*.

"Does that stand for June or January?" I asked.

"Exactly. I'm allowed to guess within two months of their actual birth month, so this evens out the odds," Patricia said. "Look, who cares? No one's going to come. And if they do, tell them the guesser's on a break."

"Then why did you explain all this to me?"

"You asked," she said. "Well, can you do it or not?"

I looked around me. Well, what were the chances of anyone coming over anyway?

"Okay," I said. "But don't take too long. I have to go home soon."

As soon as Patricia left, I studied the wording on the plank: the fine print did state that the guesser could guess the birth month within two months, age within two years, or weight within five pounds. It was a strange scam. I simply sat on the chair and watched as people passed by, many of them curious for about two seconds before they moved on to more interesting sights. As a lark, I actually started guessing in my head what people's weights, ages, and birth months were. But all that flew right out of my head when a middle-aged couple stopped in front of me to take stock of the setup.

"Howdy," the man said. He had a white beard and wore a cowboy hat. His companion was dressed in all black with so much silver jewelry on her arms I was surprised it wasn't weighing her down.

"Hi," I said. That fantasy I had of me trying to actually guess was short-lived, so I decided to take the easy way out. "The guesser's on a break," I added.

"Oh?" said the woman.

"The guesser's on a break," the man echoed, mockingly.

The woman pulled a dollar out of her small black purse and held it out.

I started to sweat. This whole day was a terrible series of awkward moments.

"I don't think he wants to take your dollar, sweetie," the man said. "Maybe we should let it be."

"No," the woman said with conviction. "He's *going* to take my dollar."

The woman had this severe look on her face that made me realize there was no way out.

"You better take the dollar, son. Marguerite doesn't take no for an answer."

Reluctantly, I took the dollar, dreading what would come next.

"Can I guess your birth month?" I said, painfully aware Patricia hadn't left me her little scribble. But I couldn't imagine this lady wanted me to guess her age or weight.

"No, I want you to guess how long I have to live," she said.

"Marguerite," the man protested.

I remained motionless, staring into her eyes. There was something vaguely familiar about that look. It wasn't fear or fury. It was more like pain. I had seen that look in my mother many times before her death. She had been dead only two years. My father, devastated by the loss, decided to start over with a new family, and left my brother and me with our grandparents. Being orphaned and abandoned during puberty left me wallowing in unanswered questions, wobbling into adolescence without guidance. I didn't want to blame my parents, but their absence left me without an important resource. I would have to stumble through my teenage years. I suppose that everyone feels that way, even with parents within reach. Yet mine was the certainty that my mistakes would be committed without the possibility of parental rescue.

"Marguerite," the man said again. He tugged delicately at her arm, but she wouldn't budge.

At that moment, everything around us disappeared. The music, the shouting, the laughing, the lights, the energy of bodies and mechanical beasts—all of it faded into a haze as the stale air thickened over my eyes. Perhaps the woman's purpose was to hand over something she didn't want anymore and the only way to do that was to teach me some life lesson I was still too green to handle, a kind of cruelty I had been subjected to all day. At fourteen years old, I didn't know very much about sex or love, but I did already know something about death. Marguerite had picked on the wrong pimple-faced kid for that, that's for sure, and I was about to let her know it, give back what she had just forced on me. And so, the following words bubbled out of my mouth, which surprised all three of us: "No more than a year, maybe two."

If there had been some possibility of persuading Marguerite to take pity on me and back off, I had just spoiled it. Her pained look turned to anger.

"What? What do you mean by that? What do you know that I don't know? How dare you say that to me? Are you hearing this little shit?"

The man took hold of Marguerite more forcibly this time and led her away. He looked back at me suspiciously, and I didn't know how to interpret that expression. All I had to say in my defense was that I knew what a dying woman looked like; I had seen one once before.

The noise of my surroundings became audible again, as if someone had turned the volume back up. A few seconds later, Patricia came back, flaunting a fresh hickey, bright as a wound, on her neck. She knew right away that something had gone down.

"Hey, what happened? Let me guess, you pissed somebody off?"

I didn't answer. Instead, I ran into the crowd, losing myself in other people's reverie, the river of bodies that were here to have a good time while the carnival was in town, before it packed up and shipped off to another county, leaving everyone to their small, everyday lives. I wanted the comfort of familiar faces, so I went to look for the others, including my cousin Vero, who would die in her early thirties, just months after the death of my cousin the Future Farmer of America, just a few years after the deaths of my grandmother, my grandfather, my father, my uncle. I didn't know this then, but I would outlive them all, leaving me all alone to tell the tale about how our paths converged at the National Date Festival with Marguerite's. Her dollar flew out of my hand during my run, discarded like a ticket stub that was still good for a single ride. Someone must have picked it up. Someone must have spent it. I guess.

ABOUT WOMEN

My brother and I had been interacting all these years because we were related, because we shared a common loss—the death of our mother, abandonment by our father—and because our grandmothers had reinforced a sense of unity. "There's only two of you," they said at different times. But during adolescence, I withdrew into a depression that our family members called shyness, and my brother began to act out, becoming just another troubled youth in that neighborhood where the adults were farmworkers and many of their sons were gang members. My brother never joined a gang, but Abuelo saw my brother's behavior as evidence to the contrary. Alex had been ditching classes more often, and hanging out with the high school dropouts, who kept him out late at night and introduced him to beer and smokes. This included a few of our cousins who never adapted to life in the U.S. and so became wage-earning laborers, which also gave them permission to make independent choices like partying late into the night even though they still lived with their parents. By this time, I had already gone away to college, and I would get distressing reports from my grandmother about Alex's fights with Abuelo. And at one time, she even suggested I let him move in with me.

"There's only two of you," she said over the phone, reaching for that simple phrase that didn't require further justification.

"But it's not that simple," I tried to explain. And it wasn't. I had left the Coachella Valley with its sad memories and its sad people. The only thing I took with me was the duty to check in on the family once in a while, to listen to them and then let them go as soon as I hung up the phone. That included my brother, who had drifted away from me since the death of our mother. He refused to invoke her memory, even her name. So I moved forward on the path of grief on my own. There were only two of us who understood that loss, and one of us wasn't talking.

"Can't he go with my father?" I suggested.

The silence that followed betrayed the terrible truths of that statement: I had defied my duty as my brother's protector, and we had become desperate enough for an alternative that we turned to the man who, a year into widowhood, found a widow with three sons. He eventually remarried and moved on without us.

"I guess there's no other choice," Abuela said, solemnly.

At sixteen years old, my brother left school and moved in with our father, who had relocated to Mexicali, just south of the border. The distance between us grew, and so did our silence for the next five years. As I focused on my studies, on new friendships and romantic relationships, I became less and less interested in Abuela's reports about the goings-on in the González family. The only time I perked up was when she told me my brother had shacked up with a young woman. I became excited by the idea of Alex finally settling down, so I resolved to go to Mexicali and meet my new "sister-in-law." I was already in graduate school in Davis at the time, and a generous fellowship had allowed me to send my brother funds to furnish his new home with Azucena. There was even poetry in her name—it meant "lily"—and I began to shape a romantic image of this young woman who had decided to make a home with my beloved brother. I imagined her as pretty as her name, a lovely scent about her, and her voice so soft and delicate that I would have to bend my ear toward her to listen. On the way there, I even bought a hefty pile of women's clothing to express my gratitude for my brother's rescue. I beamed as I imagined myself stepping into a scene so common in those fantasy love stories on Mexican telenovelas: a young couple stumbling around in a room like a pair of turtledoves because the shared space was new, the intimacy was addicting, and all they had to do was get drunk on their own voices. It was a cheesy expectation, but I needed to place my brother inside something different than in the spaces that had become, sometimes reluctantly, his homes. But then came the letdown.

The history of this piece of land in the outskirts of Mexicali was another example of how members of the González family couldn't bear living apart, no matter how much they annoyed each other. With no running water and weak electricity, this isolated place was called El Rancho, though there was nothing ranch-like about it—no animals, no farmland. It was just a long stretch of dirt with an outhouse and a small two-bedroom house that belonged to the man who had married my aunt, my father's only sister. On our many visits to the border, we had eventually end up in El Rancho because the space gave us a sense of freedom. The adults would stand around a grill and talk while the kids would play in the small canal nearby if it wasn't overflowing with irrigation water. These times were actually pleasant, and I caught a rare glimpse of what it was like to be part of a happy family. The rest of the time, the family was busy battling each other over petty things like gossip and money. Perhaps El Rancho's association with the good times is what encouraged my uncle to sell pieces of this land to his in-laws. It seemed like a profitable venture since the land was at least a decade away from development and his own children expressed no interest in ever living there. He divided the land into three properties, and sold one to Abuelo, one to my father, and one to Tío Rafael, my father's brother. Unlike the man who had sold this property, the González men did envision making homes there for themselves and for the generations to come. I knew it was yet another way for them to stay within shouting and fighting distance of one another. This was confirmed when I finally made my way to El Rancho to meet Azucena.

My bus arrived in Calexico, and then I used a pay phone to call my brother at the gas station where he worked. Since he was the manager, it was relatively easy for him to announce his early departure. Still, I had to wait at least an hour in that stuffy bus station with its coin-operated bathroom door and a snack bar that sold Mexican candy and flour-based *chicharrones* that glowed an unsavory orange. I had my portable cassette player to drown out the noise and a book to block my view of the strange dramas that unfolded in places like these, usually fights with the man behind the counter about luggage.

I was still confused about why my grandparents had chosen to move down to El Rancho after they retired. El Rancho was so removed from the paved roads, from the nearest supermarket, that any errand was an inconvenient car ride away. But after many years of living in government housing, units so compressed they were more like prison cells than homes, a house in the middle of nowhere was better than an apartment squeezed in between two others. And although El Rancho now had running water, it still had no drainage pipes. I wasn't looking forward to using the outhouse.

When my brother suddenly popped into the bus station, I jumped out of the seat in the waiting room. I had not seen my brother in over a year, yet there was no affectionate exchange, not even a handshake. That was the González way.

"How was your trip?" my brother asked as we walked to his car. He carried the heavy bag of clothes I had brought for Azucena.

"Fine," I said. "Tired as fuck though." Since we were now crossing the border, I switched to my native Spanish. He laughed and that pleased me because it made me believe everything was going to be all right.

But everything was not all right. As soon we pulled into El Rancho, I was stunned by the other changes. The canal had been filled in but there was still no road. The population had exploded, but mainly by residents who lived in shoddy shacks. The path to El Rancho was lined by the poverty I thought we had abandoned long ago. And now my family had moved right back in. The car stirred the dust into clouds, and even though the air-conditioning didn't work, we still had to close the windows, locking ourselves in with the heat. But the truth was I appreciated the haze of dirt, how it covered up the reminders of México's Third World reality.

My arrival was anticlimactic. I wasn't received with hugs or kisses. In fact, I walked into my brother's house and was met with complete indifference. Azucena looked like a bored teenager, and when my brother introduced me, she simply looked up from the couch in front of the television and then turned back to her show. This display of coldness became even more awkward when I turned over the bag of clothing I had brought for her. She took it and walked away to sift through its contents in the privacy of her bedroom.

I looked at my brother, who was seething with rage.

"She's a bitch," he said. His face darkened as he proceeded to tell me all of her faults, all of his regrets, everything stemming from the fact that a year into their union she hadn't become pregnant.

"She wants something to do," he said, and I looked around the unkempt house and understood that her behavior was one big passive aggressive gesture. I had nothing to offer by way of consolation, so we opened up a few beers and started drinking, small-talking about the old days in El Rancho. It felt good to fill up the hollowness with something.

The new days in El Rancho stank. Maybe they always did, but as a child I never noticed. The outhouses smelled; so did the pits in the back that everyone used to burn garbage. And then there was a strange, acidic odor in the air that Alex said was the chicken farm where our stepmother worked inseminating chickens.

"They used needles, you know," he said. "I should ask Amelia to bring me one and I can impregnate Azucena."

I laughed at his vulgar joke, though I could feel the disappointment in his voice. This house was empty. Meanwhile, a few doors down, my father had populated his home with three stepsons and one daughter, my half sister. I forced myself to visit, only to be met with the same disinterest. My father's stepsons were still boys, and they chased each other around the house making farting noises. My stepmother asked me a few noncommittal questions and then went back to her chores. My half sister, only about six or seven, simply stared at me, not with curiosity but with suspicion.

"What's her name?" I asked, and I immediately regretted doing that. I knew her name. Nancy. But this was my way of wounding my father, of letting him know how little I cared about his new life and family.

My father shirked off my immaturity and started spinning his usual stories. Amelia soon joined in, bantering with him in such an amusing manner that I understood immediately how well suited they were for each other. They teased each other and cut each other off with laughter. It was such a different interaction than the one I had grown up seeing with my mother, who always had too many tears and frowns. Amelia was the opposite of my mother; she was a big joyful presence with her hearty laugh and big chest. Her levity was contagious, and soon her sons joined in the fun. I listened and offered up a weak smile from the corner of the room, aware that I had nothing to contribute to this household and that a plate of food on the table was the only affection they would ever show me and that I would ever accept.

But just as quickly, I became angry at my father because whatever wisdom he had about relationships wasn't making its way to my brother. It was then that I understood why Alex had decided to find a partner—to leave my father's house.

"It was always too noisy," he said to me later when I asked him about it. "There's a happiness there that didn't include me." And I knew exactly what he was talking about.

My visit to Tío Rafael was a brief exchange through the fence. Divorced and a deadbeat father, he had moved out of the country to avoid paying child support for his three children. His ex-wife had since remarried, but he was afraid to return to the U.S., so he formed a common-law marriage with a woman who worked to support his whims. There were many false starts, however, and we witnessed him chasing after a series of women before he met Mari, the only one who could stand living in isolation, with only my temperamental uncle for company. Abuela once told me that he announced to the entire neighborhood when one of his conquests went sour because he would crank his stereo system all night and drink away his sorrows until dawn. Finally hitched, he avoided socializing with anyone except for my father and Abuela, who were the only ones he allowed into his house.

My grandparents hadn't changed much. They kept busy with a lively garden and a menagerie of dogs and parakeets. They never had any kind words to say about Amelia or her brood, and they pointed out repeatedly what a terrible decision my brother had made in moving in with a girl who didn't cook or clean.

"And apparently she doesn't fuck either," Abuelo said, rubbing his mustache. "Not even a belly after all this time. Then why keep her around?"

Instead of chiding him for his crassness, Abuela nodded in agreement. "He should throw that one away. Find another one."

"And you?" Abuelo asked. "When are you getting married? Whatever happened to that Chinese girl you were seeing?"

"Vikki," Abuela said. "How's Vikki?"

I blushed. My father hadn't even bothered asking about my love life. And my grandparents held on to some fantasy they created when I came home to visit with my friend Vikki from college. We had been having sex, but neither of us saw a future in the relationship because her parents wanted her to marry a Chinese man and, with the exception of Vikki, I only desired men. We were college companions and not much else. But when she insisted on tagging along the next time I visited my grandparents because she wanted to try homemade Mexican food, I knew her presence was going to mislead them. They were so pleased with my choice of girlfriend and displayed such a newfound respect for me that I began to convince myself that maybe this was the correct path to follow.

On the drive back to college, I dared say out loud, "Hey, Vikki, why don't we just get married? I mean, when we're done with school."

Vikki scrunched her face and said, "Why? To make your grandparents happy? You said so yourself, there's no such a thing as a happy marriage in your family. Maybe you *are* like all the other men and you're incapable of being alone. No way; you're not using me like that."

Her rebuke sobered me up, and I never proposed such a crazy idea again, though for months after that, I looked for signs during our lovemaking for a change of heart.

"She's doing fine," I said. "She moved back in with her parents."

From the corner of my eye, I caught a glimpse of a photograph of Vikki that Abuela had on display atop the television. Oh, brother, I thought. I should have never sent her that.

Back at my brother's house, Azucena only smiled once, and very faintly, when I complimented her cooking. The rest of the time, she disappeared into the television or her bedroom. She didn't surrender anything more than that single facial gesture. I tried to engage her repeatedly in conversation, but she responded by shrugging, or by pretending she hadn't heard. Frustrated, I simply gave up, and when my brother was at work, the heaviness of the silent treatment was so maddening that I chose to sit outside in the hot weather, reading as the sweat collected beneath the lenses of my glasses. I would hear the voices of my father and stepmother from two doors away—hers always punctuated by a chuckle. Once I had enough of the heat, I decided to walk back inside. When I reached the door, Azucena had locked it. She had done this deliberately, I was certain of it. But I refused to knock. I went back to my reading spot and endured a few more hours of exile, until my brother came home.

To my relief, my stay wasn't longer than a few days. I had decided to travel down to Michoacán to visit my maternal grandparents, so my brother dropped me off at the bus station. I had never made that trip alone before, and the feeling of independence was exhilarating. I took a small duffle bag, some extra cash to leave to my maternal grandmother, and a camera I borrowed from Azucena.

"I'll be back in a week," I told my brother. He nodded his head and drove off to his job across the border.

My visit to Michoacán was uneventful. Unlike the González clan, the Alcalás were low-maintenance and little drama. They went to church, ate their meals quietly, and spoke softly as they watched the afternoon darken from the chairs they set out in the garden. If there was a burst of laughter, it was nothing close to the cackling I had just heard at my father's house. And if there was sadness, it was handled with dignity. After the second day, I was bored out of my mind. I began to take short trips to the nearby towns and visit distant relatives, who were always shocked that I had dared to travel alone. "So dangerous," I kept hearing, followed by horror stories that took place on the road—bus plunges, highway robberies. Everywhere I went, I was asked about my father and my brother, and I kept repeating the same news: they had both become partnered.

"To good women?" I was asked.

"I think so," I said, but I didn't elaborate, and no one expected me to. Instead, they seized the moment to ask me about my marital plans.

"I'm still in school. I'll think about it after I graduate." I blushed each time I said that.

In the evenings, I slipped out to visit one of my old lovers. He was married now, but that didn't stop us from sneaking around in his house, sometimes while his wife was asleep with their baby. Most of the time, our sex was muffled; other times, he grunted without fear of being caught, as if this was some sort of unspoken arrangement they had made to keep the marriage intact. I suspected as much by the way he didn't rush to put his clothes back on again. And by how he rolled over, resting calmly while leaving himself completely exposed. When I tried to rest my hand on his chest, he gently pulled it off, and my fingers tingled as they waved good-bye to his hairy torso.

"I need to catch my breath," he said.

"That's fine," I said. "I wasn't asking for anything more."

"Shhh," he said. "She might hear us."

I sighed. A minute later, he was sound asleep, so I picked myself up and left as quietly as I had entered. That was the arrangement. As I walked out of the house, I heard his wife comforting their baby. The baby made gurgling noises, and suddenly I was filled with such shame that I resolved not to return—a promise I knew that I couldn't keep because my lover's pull was strong. The next afternoon, when he walked past my grandparents' house, he whistled a tune and my body leaned forward instinctively because it was getting called.

On one occasion, I was sneaking back into my grandparents' house when Abuela Herminia called out to me in the dark. She had been waiting for me in the living room.

"Where were you?" she commanded. It was an accusatory tone that had never been directed toward me.

"Abuela," I whispered. "What are you doing up? It's late."

"I asked you a question. You're in my house—I have a right to know."

"I was out with friends."

"Were you drinking?" she asked sharply.

I almost giggled but held back. "No."

"Were you smoking?"

"No, I swear it."

By now my eyes had adjusted to the dark. I could see her graying hair catching the moonlight. I became uncomfortable. I knew what was coming.

"Were you sinning?"

The scent of sex was still strong on my body. My lover's kisses, his tongue, those exploratory fingers he had inserted inside me— all the evidence of his touch now glowed in the dark, and I was convinced my grandmother could see if not catch the odor of my sinning. I hesitated in answering, and this angered her.

"I asked you a question: were you sinning? Were you sleeping with a woman?"

In the wording, I caught sight of an escape, a window that would allow me to answer the question without telling her the truth.

"No, Abuelita," I said. "I wasn't sinning with a woman. That's the truth."

She sighed in relief. Her tense posture relaxed. "Go to bed, then. And no more staying out late as long as you're here. It's dangerous."

I walked away and left her sitting in the living room. She mumbled her prayers, and that brought a heaviness on me that sunk me into a deep sleep. When I woke up the next day, my body ached because I had not removed my clothes.

Later in the week, I made my obligatory visit to my mother's grave and brought a bouquet of red gladiolas and, as a symbolic gesture, a second bouquet of white lilies as if to connect my mother to Azucena, her daughter-in-law. I wanted to tell her what had taken place since the last time I came to see her, but it was too depressing. So I simply cleaned the blue tiles of her grave and wept before I left. When I finally said good-bye to the Alcalá family, I was relieved to be leaving them also. It became clear to me then that the problem was me, not my families—I was the one who refused to join in and blend in. I was much more comfortable journeying on my own. They didn't know who I was, but neither did I reveal that to them. The secret of my sexuality was still keeping us apart. I pressed my head against the glass window of the bus in resignation. I had to make one more stop in Mexicali before heading back to college. Each day was one day closer to the world in another language that I had built without them.

Since El Rancho didn't have telephone service yet, I walked out of the Mexicali bus station and took an expensive taxi ride to El Rancho. I was feeling triumphant that I had survived my solo journey to the homeland, and as I tossed around in the backseat of the taxi, I took stock of the gifts I had brought back. I played with a pair of ornate earrings I was planning to give Azucena. I was determined to win her over yet. There was very little to report to my father and to Alex about the Alcalá family, so I congratulated myself in choosing to travel to the nearby towns instead, visits that always pleased my father to listen to. But when the car finally pulled up to my brother's house, I knew something had changed.

"Did you bring that camera?" my brother said as soon as I stepped out of the taxi. I handed it over to him. He checked that I had removed the film. Satisfied that I had, he tossed it full force over the fence.

"Why did you do that?"

"She's gone," he said. "I want nothing here that's hers."

I was so flustered by the news that I wasn't fazed by the fact that Amelia's sons were hanging around in my brother's kitchen. I refused to speak in Spanish though, because this conversation was private.

"What happened?" I asked.

"It was over a long time ago, anyway, so she was looking for an excuse to get out and she found one."

"What?" I asked. "That you weren't conceiving?"

My brother turned away from me. "No," he said. "You."

"Me? What the fuck did I do?"

"I told you she was just a bitch. She said she didn't like you. Even after all you've done for us, and all the clothes you brought her." He took a breath. "What a bitch."

"I still don't understand," I said. "Did she elaborate?"

Alex rummaged in the refrigerator for a few items. "You hungry? You want me to cook you something to eat?"

"Sure," I said. My stepbrothers watched us go about our business in silence. I wanted them to leave, but I didn't know how to tell them without sounding rude.

"Do they just hang around here now that you're single?" I said.

The clanging of pans drowned out his response.

"I still don't get it, Alex," I insisted. "What exactly did she say? What were her exact words?"

That's when my brother froze, as if considering whether to tell me. When he finally turned to me, he said, "Look, you don't need to hear it. She's gone and that's all there is to it. All I can say is that I had to choose between my brother and my woman and, well, I made my choice."

"But that's stupid, Alex; we don't even live in the same country anymore. She left and now you're alone. I'm not staying here to keep you company. I'm no longer part of your everyday life."

"Yes, you are," Alex said. "You're my brother. And no one talks shit about my bro, not even my woman. You understand what I'm saying? You're my brother and I accept you as you are. Fuck everyone else."

A warm rush came over me because I finally understood that Azucena had seen in me what my father and grandparents and even my brother had refused to see or name. Even worse, she had used that as a weapon, as an excuse to hurt my brother. I felt a renewed sense of love for Alex. I dug into my duffle bag and pulled out the pair of earrings.

"Take these to your mother," I said to the boys. "Tell her I picked them out just for her." One of them snatched the earrings and ran out of the house, and the others chased after him.

"Fried chicken okay with you?" Alex said.

"Perfect," I said.

Only the two of us now, we sat in silence as he marinated the chicken with mustard and pepper. But suddenly my brother blurted out with conviction, "Women. Who needs them anyway?"

I thought about my mother, my father's quick remarriage, my uncle's desperate search for a woman after he divorced his wife—one disappointment after another that he would drown out in alcohol until he met Mari. I thought about Vikki and my impulsive fantasy of surrendering to this notion of heterosexual happiness that for the González men was limned with heartbreak. I thought about my poor brother, devastated by his first venture into that González tradition of finding and then failing to keep a mate. My eyes watered. I had no idea what my brother was thinking about, but his eyes watered too. Who needs women? The González men certainly behaved like they didn't.

Less than a year later, he told me over the phone that he had found someone else. "What is her name?" I asked.

"Guadalupe."

"Guadalupe," I repeated. Such poetry in her name.

A Complicated Man

*D*o you remember . . . ? my father liked to ask, quite unexpectedly, usually breaking the silence in the room or in the car. *Do you remember your mother? Do you remember Zacapu? Do you remember that time we went to Disneyland?* These were not meant to start a conversation; they were more like musings. Lost in the geographies of his daydream, he would suddenly realize I was within earshot, and so I became his temporary anchor to the waking world. I would answer with a simple *Yes* and then he would drift into thought again. Except that on this second journey, he would take me with him because I did indeed remember and so I followed him through the now-lighted corridors of memory.

My father was diagnosed with Parkinson's disease in 2000, though we had long suspected there was something wrong. We had observed him slow down over time, but we had blamed it on the years of alcohol abuse, on the grief of widowerhood, and, after his second marriage, on the years of distress over his oldest stepson, who had become involved with drugs, fathering children he refused to recognize. This was also the year of the birth of Alex's first child, Halima—a name I had picked out, and that Guadalupe loved. "It's Arabic," I explained. "It means something like *she who sings and dances even in times of sorrow.*" So I made it a point to visit

Alex and his family more often, now that the baby brought renewed peace to his household. As with his previous union, the inability to conceive had troubled his relationship. But somehow, this miracle happened. I had moved to New York City a few years prior and didn't have the money or the time to make the long trek across the country, so my communication with Alex had been over the phone.

"So much has changed. Maybe now's the perfect time to come," he said.

I borrowed money from my boyfriend at the time, and bought a plane ticket to LA. And then I took the bus from LA to the border—a lengthy, uneventful ride through the desert. Traveling though the Coachella Valley, however, brought back the memories, pleasant and devastating. It was a feeling I didn't get from visiting Michoacán anymore, because southern California had become my new homeland. When the bus dove past the vineyards of the little town of Thermal, I had the urge to point out to anyone who would listen that my father had razed this land where the vineyards grew. And those onion fields on the left, my family had harvested those each summer. But I suspect these were not unusual stories to anyone on board since we were all Mexicans headed to the U.S.-México border. No one was excluded from the farmworker stories. As we spilled out of the bus in Calexico, Alex was already waiting for me at the station.

When I arrived at El Rancho, I became nervous about the kind of reception I would get from Guadalupe, but my fears were assuaged before I even stepped out of my brother's car. Guadalupe met us at the gate, cheerful and vibrant, holding Halima in her arms. And when I noticed my niece was wearing the miniature version of her mother's shoes, I gushed with giddiness.

"How was your journey, brother?" she said, handing me the baby, and I almost wept with gratitude. I was also pleased to see that she took good care of my brother: something spicy was cooking on the stove, the living room was tidy, the laundry room was orderly and neat—nothing like the chaos I had encountered when Alex was living with Azucena.

Since it was customary to pay my respects to the elders, I didn't let too much time pass before I said my quick hellos to my uncle and my grandparents. That's when I realized how much had not changed. The complaints were nonstop: my grandfather said my stepbrothers played their music too loudly; my uncle said my brother kept cutting down too many branches off the tree they shared; my uncle's second wife, Mari, said my stepbrothers parked the cars too close to their lot; my grandfather said Mari kept flooding the yards; Mari said my sister-in-law was letting the dogs dig into the fence they shared; my grandmother kept pointing out incessantly how late Guadalupe slept in after my brother went off to his shift at the gas station at five in the morning. I thought about how much wiser the Alcalá family had always been—each unit living in a different town, close enough to visit but far enough to maintain privacy.

No one actually expected me to do anything but listen since I was not there to offer solutions or take sides. I was simply a fresh set of ears, the family member who hadn't heard the thorough account of what was going on. And without exception, each run-down was punctuated with the threat of leaving the González neighborhood, though I knew no one would ever dare.

The only evident change was that everyone was getting older and weaker. Tío Rafael had suffered a stroke that left him bound to a wheelchair, though this did nothing to tame his temper. In fact, it worsened, enraged by the fact that he couldn't express his discontent the way he used to—storming out of a room or hurling objects against the wall. Now he simply tensed up and cursed his luck, imploding within the confines of the metal. The only saving grace was that the old generation of farmworkers—my retired grandparents, my uncle, and now my father, who began to collect disability insurance—was finally having its rest. But now they sat around and drove each other crazy.

I skipped my father's house. Alex had warned me there was a feud between Guadalupe and Amelia, and in this case my loyalty was to my brother's household.

"Apá will come around anyway," my brother assured me. We sat outside the house drinking beer. I had arrived in the summer, and it was cooler outside with the breeze than inside with the wimpy ceiling fan. Plus, Guadalupe had just taken the baby in for a nap, and I didn't want to disturb her rest with our talking.

Just then our half sister Nancy, a teenager now, walked in front of the house, holding a little girl by the hand.

"Is that our beloved father's granddaughter?" I asked Alex, referring to the toddler.

"Well, not really," Alex said. "I thought I had mentioned it before."

I turned to Alex. "What do you mean?"

He started laughing. "That's actually your second sister."

"What the fuck?" I almost dropped the beer in my hand. "Are you kidding me?"

"Nope. Hey, don't feel bad, he didn't tell me either. I think he was too embarrassed or something."

I shook my head in disbelief. My father was in his midforties, my brother was in his late twenties, and both of them had baby girls.

"What's her name?" I asked.

"Laura."

The name did nothing for me. And neither did the revelation that I had a second sister. If the birth of the first one didn't please me, I was completely indifferent to the news of the second. I only hoped that he was being a father to his daughters in ways he hadn't been a father to his sons.

Despite the fact that Nancy had not even bothered to wave

hello, it was clear she had seen me and reported back to my father, because a few moments later, Alex spotted him walking over.

"Brace yourself; here comes our father," Alex said. "Just don't lend him any money, Turrútut. He'll drink it."

Watching my father walk the few yards from the gate to the front door of the house was devastating because he now moved in slow motion, using a cane for support. Alex had prepared me for what to expect: he had a slight limp and was losing muscle control over his arms and head, a side effect of the cheap medication he could afford with his disability insurance. Since he could not feed himself well, he was losing weight, but he was stubborn as ever about his drinking and refused to quit.

As he walked up to us, I began to suspect that he was exaggerating his debilitated gait as a strategy to disarm me. We had little to no communication over the years. I never called him and he never called me. No message was ever delivered through my brother, who didn't give me updates on my father's family because I didn't want them. That was why the news of his second daughter remained unspoken until now. I didn't really care to know. When he finally made it to the porch, my father came up to me and planted a kiss on my head. He smiled and kept showing his broken front tooth. This too, I thought cynically, was on purpose.

"How are things?" my father asked.

"They're fine," I said.

"That's good."

The exchange was so detached from emotion that it made me want to get up and kick something. After all these years, I had not let go of the heartbreak I felt when he abandoned us as teenagers, and that pain had turned into rage.

"How are things with you?" I asked.

"I've been sick," he said. "And so has the little one."

At the mention of his second daughter, he struck a nerve, which made me see past his disability and those distracting movements of his neck and shoulder. From the corner of my eye, I saw my brother tense up. Never one to let an opportunity to get back at my father pass me by, I seized on it.

"I don't see how your little one is my responsibility," I said. "She's your child, not mine."

"But she's your sister," my father pushed back. "Just like Nancy."

"Are you hearing this man?" I turned to my brother, which was my way of pressuring him to side with me, though I knew he wouldn't. Since he had been living close to my father all those years, he had an opportunity to repair some of the damage in the relationship. I didn't have that advantage.

"What?" my father said. "I'm not saying anything that isn't true."

"That little one is no more my sister than you're my father," I said. "That's the truth."

My father's face darkened. I thought I heard my brother whisper something like "Calm down, Turrútut," but it did nothing to diffuse the situation.

"So you're not going to lend me any money?"

"Oh, shit," I heard my brother mutter in the back.

A scene flashed across my mind: My mother crying at the kitchen table because my father had not come home. It was payday. He would stumble in late that night, drunk and penniless. He would come over to check on me, hoping I was awake so that I would greet him with the compassion my mother didn't. But I would pretend I was asleep because that's the best way I knew how to reject him—by keeping my eyes closed.

My voice cracked as I finally mustered up the energy to respond. "I don't understand you, Apá. Didn't you learn anything from your first failure as a father? You want your drinking to ruin your second family too?"

"What do you know about me?" he said. "You abandoned me a long time ago."

"You abandoned me first! You're the one who fucked it up for all of us!"

"That's enough." My brother finally stepped in.

Like wrestlers after a scuffle, my father and I slumped in our seats in complete silence.

Sadly, this tense exchange took place each time I visited up until August 2006, the last time I saw my father alive. By then, I was numb to his pitiful pleas, especially since these became more desperate over time.

On one occasion, he had gone down to Michoacán with his family for a long overdue visit. I had nothing to say on the matter until my brother called me in New York City to tell me that my father had called him with an outlandish story.

Apparently my father had gone down to the cemetery in Zacapu, where my mother was buried, to drop off some flowers and to say hello to his former in-laws who lived nearby. My father was shocked to discover that my mother's grave was damaged and that it appeared to have been opened. When he asked my maternal grandparents about it, my grandfather confessed that my grandmother had stupidly agreed to allow someone else to be buried in that same tomb with my mother's remains. My father was beside himself, so he asked my brother to ask me to wire him the money so that he could take care of it before he left town.

"And what exactly does he plan to do?" I asked my brother.

"He says he wants to have her remains moved to the church," my brother said. "Apparently there's a wall there where people can entomb remains for a fee."

After a lengthy silence, I said, "I don't believe a word of it."

My brother was outraged. How could we let them do this to our mom? How could I not believe it? It was too bizarre to be made up! But I insisted. And to prove it, the next chance I got, I booked a flight to Mexico City, took a six-hour bus ride to Michoacán, grabbed a taxi in downtown Zacapu, and rode directly to the cemetery. My mother's grave was intact.

When I dropped in on my maternal grandparents unexpectedly, I told them about what my father had reported. They shook their heads in pity. It was true my father had come to visit them, but he came to ask them for money, and to tell them that I was the most ungrateful of his children, a college professor making good money, but that I refused to help my impoverished father all these years. I sat in silence and absorbed the rage. I held it all in until I returned to Mexicali and related to Alex what I had found.

"Are you going to let him have it?" he said. I detected some anticipation in his voice.

I did not confront my father about his lies because I knew I could not restrain myself. I was afraid I would physically attack him for manipulating our weakest point like that. My brother kept quiet about it as well, and my father simply kept coming over to his house as if he had never made that phone call.

Perhaps it was this silence, this long pretense that gave my father courage to repeat the same crazy story the following year, when he made another trip down to Michoacán and ran out of money. Since he knew my brother and I would not bail him out just like that—especially since we had heard about the extravagant parties he was throwing to impress his in-laws—when he made his phone call, he told my brother, "This time I'm telling the truth!"

When my brother told me, there was no anger in his voice this time. Only sadness. And I thought, at least my brother won't be deceived anymore. And I considered myself luckier because I didn't live two doors down from the man who had injured me.

"How do you deal with him being so close?" I once asked my brother. And my brother gave an answer so devastating that it

A Complicated Man

dried my mouth: "I just pretend he's my neighbor and not my father. It gets me through it."

Do you remember Quiroga, you?" my father asked, breaking the uncomfortable silence. He had taken a seat on an upturned bucket instead of a chair. His mustache was thin and already graying, but I couldn't imagine it would reach Abuelo's bristly stage until another decade or two. He explained that a bucket was much more comfortable for a man of his height: five foot two. He took his cane and propped his right hand over it, facing the street. On the other side, where a field of beets used to grow, a low-income housing complex was under development. The tiny units were beginning to sprout like mushrooms. My father looked the place over: a miniature king surveying a miniature kingdom.

When I didn't reply at first, my brother glared at me. I read his mind: *Don't be an asshole. Don't give him the silent treatment.*

"Yes," I responded and my mouth began to water. To remember Quiroga was to remember carnitas, the pork slow-roasted inside an oversized copper pot. La Plaza Principal is the main artery of Quiroga, and carnitas sellers line the street tempting clients with samples. Tables are provided free of charge, but patrons have to buy their own tortillas sold by enterprising Purépecha women walking about with large handwoven baskets. The pork meat, skin, and fat explode in the mouth.

Alex took a swig of his beer. I was certain he too remembered Quiroga, though he had been there only once. I had made many visits. As had my father. Those carnitas beckoned us back each time. Quiroga, Michoacán, was only a forty-five-minute bus ride from Zacapu, my father's birthplace, where my brother and I spent our childhood, where our maternal grandparents still lived. But the women who sold tortillas reminded us of Abuela María, my father's mother. She wore the same colorful aprons. She too was Purépecha, but from the village of Nahuatzen.

"Do you have carnitas in New York?" my father asked.

I wanted to say that carnitas were everywhere. I had tasted them in California, in Texas, in Chicago, and yes, even in New York City, though the only place worth ordering them was at a restaurant on the Upper West Side. Still, nowhere like Quiroga. But what made carnitas tasty in Quiroga was the place itself. The entire plaza was one large kitchen with one large dining table serving a single item. The smell clung to clothing, to hair. The taste-testing along the street was just for show. Each free sample was as delicious as the next.

"One kilo, please," a buyer will say, finally surrendering to one of the sellers. And the butcher slices and dices the meat into delicate bite sizes using a big clunky cleaver.

"No," I replied, finally. "There are no carnitas in New York." This was a fib. But it pleased my father to hear it. It made Quiroga that much more special. And it made this attempt at reconciliation much easier.

My father gave me a satisfied nod and smiled. He then turned his gaze toward the street and drifted into thought.

"He does that a lot more nowadays," Alex said to me in English, concern in his voice. After all these years, we still switched languages when we wanted to speak privately to each other.

We sat in silence for another fifteen minutes. Guadalupe popped her head out for a second and asked my father if he was staying for lunch. When he didn't reply, she simply shrugged and went back into the house, as if this wasn't the first time my father retreated so far into his head, he became lost.

Without warning, my father came to all of a sudden and said, "Well, I'll see you both later." He got up and started his slow trek back to his house.

Alex and I watched patiently as he baby-stepped out of the driveway and turned left, using his cane for balance. When a couple of schoolgirls appeared, they surpassed him easily, as did anyone else walking the same direction.

"He was never the same after the meat incident," my brother said.

"What are you talking about?"

According to Alex, to keep him feeling useful, my stepmother would send my father on small errands. One time she sent him to the butcher's to buy skirt steak. In México, the butchers wrap any purchase in clear plastic, making the item quite visible from a distance. As my father lumbered home with the meat in his hand, an opportunistic thief on a bicycle came up and simply snatched the meat from my father's grip. My father could not run after the thief and the thief knew this, mocking his victim by rolling away without even increasing his speed. It was a humiliating experience for my father, who refused to run such errands again. Now he simply walked back and forth from his house to my brother's.

Guadalupe stepped out of the house again, this time holding the sleepy child in her arms. I was still charmed by how much Halima resembled her mother. Without saying a word, Guadalupe placed the child in my brother's arms and then went inside. My brother cooed and baby-talked as the child pressed her face into his body.

"You just missed your abuelito," I said to the little girl.

My brother, quick to the punch, pointed to the street. "No, you didn't, *amorcito*. *There* he is! Wave to your abuelito."

I looked out, and indeed a body was still visible on the street. But it didn't look like my father at all, not the way I remembered him, not the way he wanted to be remembered, I was sure of this. So I took my eyes off that slow, pathetic shape of a man and stared at the sky, searching for the mountain of a man my father used to be in other towns, in other times.

We never did this as children, but as grown men, my brother and I began to lie down next to each other in bed, look up at the ceiling, and talk. It became a kind of ritual during my visits. The first time Guadalupe walked by the bedroom and saw our bodies stretched across the bed, she muttered, "You two are weird." After that, she caught on that this was a private meeting between brothers and didn't interrupt our sessions. That summer, a moment of reckoning arrived: I was going to come out to my brother.

I signaled to my brother that I was ready for one of our sessions by taking my place on the bed with the door open. As soon as he saw this, he walked in and lied down beside me.

"I really like Guadalupe," I said. "And Halima is beautiful."

"Yeah."

After a brief pause, I jumped in. "Hey, so I want your wife to be comfortable around me."

"I don't think that's going to be a problem; she's different."

"I'm glad to hear that. I can tell," I said.

Another pause.

"So I'm writing another book," I said finally. "About our family, our father, and what happened to us."

"Okay."

"But it's a book of memories. And I'm revealing all kinds of personal things."

"Like what?" Alex said.

"Well, about getting involved with drugs, about my depression."

"Okay."

"And one more very personal thing."

"What?" Alex said, but I couldn't spit it out. In fact, I began to hyperventilate to the point that my brother propped himself on his elbow to look at me. "What is it? What is it? You're scaring me."

"I—I—I'm gay!"

My brother dropped his body on the bed. "Ah, you stupid bitch, you had me worried. I thought you were going to tell me you had cancer or something. I knew you were gay since we were kids."

I started to laugh. "You did? Then why didn't you say anything?"

"Because it's not for me to say. It's for you to say. And I'm glad you finally told me. And when I told Guadalupe about it, she said she suspected as much because of the gifts you picked out for Halima. She said no straight man she ever knew had such an eye for pretty things. She doesn't care. She grew up with gay friends."

Relieved, I took a deep breath and wondered why I hadn't come out to my brother before. It was such an anticlimactic moment that it wasn't worth the wait. So I decided on another direction.

"Do you think our father knows?"

"I don't know," Alex said. "You know how it is around here. No one talks about those things. They still ask when you're getting married."

"Yeah, I know. Abuela still asks about Vikki." We chuckled together.

"But seriously, don't you think he suspects?"

"Maybe," Alex said. "I did catch him looking at your pierced ears."

I touched my earlobes. I had forgotten about them completely. They didn't make me more gay than before, but people thought they did make me *look* more gay. For the longest time, I refused to pierce my ear because every male in the family had done it— my father, my brother, Tío Rafael—so when I finally caved in, I decided to be different and pierced both.

"In any case," I said, "That's the least of our worries. We have so many other issues to work out before we even touch that one."

"I'll say," Alex said. And then he added, "So do you have a boyfriend back in New York?"

I blushed. It was going to take some getting used to.

"I do," I said. And then I talked about my love life as if it was the most normal conversation in the world, because it finally was.

—Do you remember that time we spotted each other at the plaza in Zacapu, Apá?

—I'm not sure. What trip was that?

—I was staying with my mother's family and you were staying with your wife's family.

—We always split up like that. It could have been on any trip.

—It was that time we took a bus together to Michoacán. I was nineteen. We went our separate ways, but many days later, we spotted each other.

—Did I see you?

—You didn't? I waved and I thought you waved back.

—I think I remember. Was it in front of the big cathedral, just outside the gate? Was it in the evening?

—No. It was at the bus stop across the kiosk of the smaller plaza. It was morning.

—Then I don't remember, you. Are you sure it was me?

—I'm sure. Then who was it that you were waving back to in front of the cathedral, just outside the gate that evening?

—Well, that's the funny thing, you know. I thought I was waving at you.

I had one more heated exchange with my father before I left. Alex and I were sitting in the front porch as usual, bringing up old memories of El Rancho with our cousins, when I saw my father's oldest stepson walking arm in arm with a pretty young woman. As far as anyone knew, he had fathered two children already and with no job and no education, his future wasn't very promising.

"And which of the two baby mamas is that?" I asked casually.

"Neither," Alex answered. "That's a third one."

"You're shitting me," I said.

"Nope."

"And he doesn't even pay for diapers?"

"Our father does, sometimes."

A Complicated Man

My face grew warm. So when my father came over that afternoon, I confronted him about it.

"What control do I have over that boy?" he said, visibly shaken that I had the audacity to bring it up.

"Well, you raised him," I said. "Didn't you teach him better?"

"And what business is it of yours, anyway?" he said. And I had a perfect response to this as well.

"I know you've been supplying those girls with diapers and baby formula. And then you come around asking Alex and me for money. Why should we pay for your goddamn stepson's mistakes?"

"And *you're* perfect? At least he's giving me grandchildren. Between the two of you, I've only gotten one, and she's probably the only one I'll ever get to see!"

"You respect my brother," I said. "At least he's not a fuckup like your stepsons."

"Sons who love their father. Do you love yours?"

"I don't have a father!" I said.

That's when my brother got up from his seat and stood between us, as if our father and I could actually come to blows. Alex told us to be quiet, that we were dishonoring his house. He told our father to go home and he told me to cool off in the guest room. When Alex came by to check on me, I was in tears.

"Turrútut, I just can't stand to even see him anymore. I don't know how you do it."

"I can't stand it either sometimes," Alex said. "But I don't have a choice, do I?"

There was an accusation in his statement that stung me. But he was right. I had chosen to run away and to stay away. And when I packed my bag to head back to the U.S., it felt like an escape, and it felt so good.

By the time I was back in NYC, I was already making travel plans with college friends of mine who had moved back to

México. After dreaming about it for years, we committed finally to visiting Cuba that December.

"They won't stamp your passport if you're an American," they assured me. "Especially if you fly in from México. Everybody does it."

The arrangement sounded simple enough: we would all meet in Mexico City, buy our plane tickets in cash, and live out this bohemian fantasy. My friend from Iran was particularly eager to show me the dazzling display of cultural richness that so scared the U.S. government. As a politicized Chicano, this clandestine trip was the ultimate badge of honor since the Chicano community aligned itself philosophically with Fidel Castro. But in all honesty, I simply wanted to keep being a tourist. My modest professional success had allowed me to visit Spain, Brazil, and Costa Rica. I was excited about the next possibility, and Cuba seemed like the right place. I had invited my boyfriend to join me, but he was nervous about being caught since he was in the U.S. with a green card. "I'd rather not risk it," he said. "You go. Have fun."

At the time, I was teaching at an undergraduate college in Manhattan. Each class session was one day closer to the end of the semester and to the beginning of winter break. I was becoming obsessed with Cuba, looking up websites in my office between classes and catching up on Cuban literature. The exhilaration intensified because this was a secret trip and no one around me other than my boyfriend knew I was going.

Then one afternoon, as I walked into the apartment, my boyfriend casually said, "Hey, there's a message for you on the answering machine. I think it's your father."

I froze. "That's impossible," I said. "My father has never called me. He would never call me. He doesn't even have my number."

But sure enough, it was my father's voice on the machine, speaking a series of short, awkward sentences that didn't express alarm or concern. He was just saying hello. I immediately called Alex at work.

"I didn't think he was going to call," he said.

"But what does he want? If he starts calling nonstop, asking for money, I'm going to kill you."

"That's not why he called," my brother said confidently.

"Then why?"

"Well, I told him you were gay."

I almost fainted. "Oh my God."

"I had to, Turrútut; he kept coming over bugging me about why you had moved so far away and why you hadn't married. You basically tipped him off with your pierced ears. So I think he wanted me to confirm it. So I did. I told you had moved to New York to be with another man."

"And what did he say to that?"

"He said you had made your way through the world without him, so he had no right to say anything about it, but that he worried other people might. And then he asked me for your number. I didn't think he would call."

But he did. And I didn't feel compelled to call him back. Not right away. I had to think about what it would mean to share such intimate knowledge of myself with the man who had abandoned me when I was thirteen. That exchange became more pressing when, a few days later, as I was ready to book a flight from New York to Mexico City, I got a somber call from my brother.

"Dad's in the hospital."

"Oh, God. It's not because of the gay thing, is it?" I said.

"What are you talking about?"

"Nothing."

"It's the drinking," he said. "I think it's serious this time, Turrútut."

"Do you think I should see him?"

"It's up to you if you want to come," Alex said. "I know it's been rough. I've got his number at the hospital if you want to call him first."

My body contracted. I didn't want to call my father. I was afraid that the first thing out of his mouth was going to be a plea for reconciliation. And I needed to work a few things through before I even thought about a reunion.

"Let me think about it," I said. "Can I call you again tomorrow to talk about it some more?"

I called my brother every day for a week, going back and forth on whether I was going to call, let alone visit. During that time, my father's health improved, though he was now more disabled than before since he had done more damage to his liver and gall bladder. I finally did call my father on the day before he was due to be released.

"I know we haven't been good to each other," my father said. "And I want us to change. I want us to be father and son the way it should have always been. I want us to have something beautiful before I die."

My body melted on the other end of the line. There was such sincerity in his voice that I believed it, so I made a drastic change in my itinerary and decided to fly to California instead of Mexico City that holiday season. I postponed my trip to Cuba and prepared myself for the Big Reconciliation, what I had secretly hoped for all these years. It would happen finally. On the flight to the west coast, I felt an unburdening, as if I were stripping off chains. With the actual clouds next to me up in the sky, I couldn't shake off that I was truly inhabiting a cliché, but it was the truth: I was happily on cloud nine.

I arrived in Ontario, California, on a Saturday, and my best friend Sandra in Riverside picked me up at the airport. She had heard about the troubles between my father and me over the years, so she was glad that this lengthy battle was reaching a truce. I couldn't contain my excitement and I kept repeating, "It's enough to make me cry." I made plans to take the Greyhound bus the next morning for the three-hour ride to the international border. My brother would be waiting at the bus station in Calexico.

On the way from the airport, my friend and I decided to spend the day doing silly stuff like shopping and going to the movies since I needed some distraction. But no sooner had I finished dropping the heavy luggage in my friend's living room when my cell phone rang. It was Alex.

"Hello?"

"Hey," he said. "I've got some bad news. Our father's gone."

I went pale. What a cruel punishment. I had made up my mind to see my father, to let go of all the resentment and pain, to travel across the country, only to discover I had arrived too late. Maybe this was the cosmic payback, some higher power's way of letting me know I had paved my own path toward tragedy via my pride and wrath—two of the unforgivable deadly sins. I would now have to carry this new burden through the rest of my days. I was never meant to walk the earth without some huge psychological weight over my shoulders.

"When did he die?" I asked.

"Die?" my brother said, sounding confused. "He didn't die. He chickened out on the reunion and took off to Michoacán."

I had to reposition my emotions before I started yelling into the phone.

I became so disoriented, I lost my balance and collapsed on the floor. I told my brother I was still planning to go down to see him and my niece, and I left it at that. But when I let it all out in front of my friend, she was stunned, not at my father's audacity but at the intensity of my rage. I was on the verge of a breakdown. I could feel my skull cracking and I pictured my brain bubbling like lava. For the rest of the day, my body trembled.

That night, I didn't sleep, and I concentrated on the rattling of the ceiling fan, hoping the fixture would dislodge and send the blades hurling down like a propeller to shred my body. I drank an entire bottle of wine before getting into bed. Eventually the tears stopped and I fell asleep. By the time my brother picked me up at the bus station on the border the next day, I had hardened myself more than before: never again.

The following year, Abuelo passed away in the spring after a yearlong stroke-induced paralysis. I had seen him briefly on my last visit to El Rancho, and the damage to his facial muscles and speech was evident. He had just been released from a surgery to clear an artery, and there he was, sweeping his front porch, wearing his hospital gown and identification bracelet like badges of honor.

"That man is going to outlive us all," I commented to my brother.

But a few months after the surgery, my grandfather suffered another stroke. This time, he was left unable to swallow or speak. I received updates from my brother all year long: he's now hospitalized in California; his hair is completely white; he's thinned down, almost skeletal; he's now in a convalescent home; my grandmother attempted to feed him a burrito and he almost choked.

"Why did she do that?" I asked. "Didn't she know it was dangerous?"

"She said she felt sorry for him. You know Abuelo's greatest pleasure was food."

Family members from Michoacán and long-lost relatives from southern California came forward to pay Abuelo a visit at the home. I was the only one who remained stubbornly at a distance, unwilling to see my grandfather in such an emaciated state. The truth was I was afraid of feeling sorry for my grandfather, or worse, of softening my emotions and setting aside all the years of torment he unleashed on most of us. It seemed unfair to expect me to show compassion to a man who was responsible for so much of my grief. I had not forgiven Abuelo for his abuse or my father for his

A Complicated Man

neglect, and I still couldn't understand how my brother could stand to live between them all these years.

If my brother held any ill will toward them, he didn't show it. He accepted his role as resident ambulance with dignity: if our grandfather didn't need a ride to the doctor, then our wheelchair-bound uncle did. Or our father. I once confessed to Alex that I never could have done any of it, not without griping. When he responded, "Well, it's family," I felt adrift at sea, straining my eyes to catch a glimpse of a landmass on which I would never set foot.

When my grandfather finally passed away, the death was anti-climactic. I felt no sense of release or catharsis. The day was like any other, except I felt a little guilty that I expressed no grief. I was the only one not present at the funeral, and if that made anyone upset, I never heard about it.

"It was sad, Turrútut," my brother informed me over the phone. "No one cried."

The point of comparison, I believed, was our mother's funeral, which had been gushing with grief and tears.

"And then the priest really blew it," my brother continued, "by going on and on about what a good man had left the earth, how he had given his family years of happiness and shit like that."

"How did the others react?" I asked.

"How do you think? People could barely contain their laughter. The only reason we didn't burst was out of respect for our grand-father's sisters who showed up. But even Abuela rolled her eyes."

Right after the burial, my grandmother withdrew the money from all the bank accounts and then locked herself in her house with ten dogs in the yard to keep the rest of us out. There wasn't much money in those three or four accounts my grandparents kept open over the years. Once I asked them why they did that, spread the money around like that, and Abuelo answered, "Well, what if somebody robs the bank with all our money in it?"

"She asked me to take her to Abuelo's grave before we left,"

Alex said. "She stood over it for a few seconds and then said, 'You stay there, you,' before she walked away."

Although we fantasized that the day Abuelo died, Abuela would blossom in her newly found freedom, she disappointed us by becoming a recluse, locked up in her house and refusing to take any visitors. Even when I called on her during my rare trips to El Rancho, she would only speak to me through the fence, and I would have to hold my tongue as she launched her complaints against Guadalupe and accused my brother of stealing money from her.

Alex took it all in stride. "She's getting old and senile, Turrútut. I'm not going to hold anything against her."

In moments like these, I wondered if my brother and I were actually related. He had this incredible capacity for sympathy toward those around him that I didn't. Maybe because I wasn't around them, because all I had taken with me were the terrible memories of the past. He had remained among them, experiencing the narrative grow into something more complex, more human, more worthy of understanding.

Once, on our way to the liquor store to pick up more beer, my brother and I were riding down the street in his truck when I casually pointed out that the old lady walking though the dusty road at high noon looked like our grandmother.

"That *is* our grandmother," he responded.

"What?" I said, in alarm. "Then let's pick her ass up; she's going to get heat stroke out there!"

"She won't get in the truck, Turrútut," my brother said, somberly. "I've tried it before."

And when we passed her by, I nearly burst into tears. I watched her tiny body become tinier still, and I felt such pity for the family we had become. My heart was heavy with sadness, because the stories I wanted to remember her by were the sentimental ones, like the time she received word from Michoacán that Mamá Lola, her mother and our great-grandmother, had died. She walked into the room while my brother and I were watching television and said through a face full of tears, "You know what? I'm an orphan too." Or like that time, on our first day of school in the U.S., when she walked my brother and me to the bus stop. She saw that we were petrified, so she offered us the only solace she could muster by informing us that the word for *ventana* in English was "window," and then she walked away. An echo of that moment came to me when I was driving solo from California to Arizona to start a graduate degree. I drove out of the housing project in my compact orange Celica at five in the morning, because I had been taught by my family to travel that way—early. She stepped out to see me off and made the sign of the cross and started to cry, and I wept all the way to the highway because it felt I had someone who would miss me the way my father never did.

"Where is she going at this hour anyway?" I asked.

"To get her beer," Alex said. "She says it's the only thing that keeps her happy anymore."

"Ain't that the truth," I said. We pulled up to the gas station and I handed Alex some money to pay for the case of twenty-four.

—I got a question for you both.

—What, Apá?

—I look at my watch and it's *dos minutos para las dos.* How do you say that in English?

—Two minutes to two o'clock. Right, Alex?

—Right.

—Okay, then what if I asked you, at that very moment, what time it was on *your* watch?

—I would say, Two minutes to two o'clock. Same as you.

—But wouldn't you say, *también*?

—Oh, I get it. Two minutes to two o'clock too!

—But isn't there a more efficient way to say it?

A Complicated Man   99

—No.

—Yes, there is, right, Apá? I get it! I get it!

Alex got it.

—You mean, Two to two too?

—Two to two too! Two to two too! Turrútut, right, Apá?

—Right, Alex. Or better yet: Right, Turrútut.

Turrútut. I liked the sound of that.

When I saw my father again in 2003, then 2004, then 2005, each visit became shorter than the one before. Forty minutes, twenty minutes, and then ten. He slipped back into the familiar pattern of greeting me, then asking me for money and making me mad. In between those annual trips to El Rancho, I felt obligated to ask my brother for updates over the phone.

"How's Apá holding up, Turrútut?"

"Depressed, Turrútut," was the usual answer.

Knowing that my father was deteriorating was painful, and every year I dreaded having to scuffle with this opponent who every year became weaker and weaker. He was having such a difficult time walking now that I suggested to my brother we get him an electric wheelchair.

"Are you nuts?" my brother said. "He'll never go for that. He's too proud."

I remembered our poor Tío Rafael. He too had been too proud once, but after his stroke, he had no choice. There was no room for shame in these matters. I had just won an arts grant the year before, so I planned to use the money on an electric wheelchair.

As predicted, my father didn't go for it. In fact, he became offended and more determined than ever to prove he was still functional, so he continued to take the car out even though he no longer had a valid license, and he refused to ease his drinking.

As my father's conditioned worsened, Alex and I had managed to get better medication, which kept my father from shaking too much, but it also slowed him down. When he ate, his movements were like a sloth's. He still refused to stop drinking, which got him in trouble once when he became temporarily paralyzed. The doctor told him he deserved it for not following instructions, and that the paralysis would wear off in a day.

"So the doctor told him to use that day to think about what will happen the next time he mixes the medication with alcohol," my brother reported.

In the summer of 2006, I received an advance copy of the childhood memoir I had been working on over the years. *Butterfly Boy: Memories of a Chicano Mariposa* recounted my tense relationship with my father up until I turned twenty. I had just turned thirty-six. I decided to share that copy with my brother but begged him not to tell my father. My father wouldn't be able to read the book in English, but neither did I want him to know it was going to be out in the world. I made a special trip to El Rancho to hand-deliver the book to Alex.

I was so nervous about that trip that I spent the three days before my arrival nursing an upset stomach. I was particularly anxious about seeing my father, as if he would be able to read in my eyes that I had betrayed him somehow by writing a book about my journey through adolescence, a coming of age made more difficult because of his absence. I didn't know it then, but that would be the last time I saw my father alive, and the exchange lasted no more than a minute. He didn't even bother with a greeting. He simply jumped right into it.

"Could you let me borrow a hundred dollars?" he said as soon as he walked in.

"No," I said. My mouth became dry. I wanted to say more, but I knew I wouldn't be able to spit another syllable out. On the coffee table sat a copy of the book, and my father didn't even notice.

He sat in silence for five minutes and then went home. I never saw him again.

"I was afraid he would see the book," I told my brother, relieved.

Alex picked it up and looked at it. "Then who did you write this for?"

The question startled me. "I guess I wrote it for us. I mean, some things are too heavy to carry by myself."

"Well, I'll tell you what I think about it. But don't call me until I call you."

For weeks after my visit, I was a wreck, waiting for my brother to tell me his response to the memoir. I had been very honest about my father's alcoholism, my relationship with an abusive lover, and my sexuality. Though I had come out to my brother many years before, he was now reading an account that showed me completely naked in other ways. When I didn't hear back from him for almost a month, I broke our agreement and called him.

"Did you finish reading the book?"

"Yeah."

"And?"

"I cried," he said.

"Well, that's understandable."

"For two days."

"Why?" I said, alarmed.

"It just brought back sad memories. About our mom."

And when I asked him if it bothered him to read all those things I wrote about our father, he simply answered, "Why should it? It's true."

"And it doesn't bother you that other people will read those things?"

"Not really. Maybe you're right. Maybe it's better for these stories to be out in the world than in our heads."

The week before I held a book launch for *Butterfly Boy* at a Manhattan bookstore, I got a call from my brother. My father had been hospitalized. I had been through this avenue before, and this time I wasn't going to slip into crisis mode, so I simply called every day to see how my father was doing. Apparently he had fallen ill over the weekend, and my brother had to drive my father across the border in the middle of the night, since my father's disability insurance could cover his medical needs. Two days later, he went into a coma, and he remained unconscious most of the time until he passed away on October 1.

During my father's coma, I received plenty of advice about whether I should go visit him, but in the end I decided not to. Not only was I going to be just another body for my brother to shuttle around, but I felt I had to save money for whatever expenses came our way. Besides my brother, there was only me to foot the bill. Our stepmother was a farmworker, and our stepbrothers held low-wage jobs in Mexicali. Although a few cousins came forward with offers of financial assistance, my brother and I decided that we were not going to take money from anyone.

That week was an emotional one for my brother and me. We debated and argued about certain decisions, like the Do Not Resuscitate form. We were so distressed that nothing came out clear and we misinterpreted our tones as defensive and hostile. In the end, I let my brother make all the decisions since it was he who was out there driving Abuela and Amelia to and from the hospital and I was back in the safety of New York City.

Five days before the book launch in New York City, my father died. I felt relief for my brother, but I felt sorry for myself. There would be no more chapters in the complex relationship between my father and me. He was now committed entirely to memory. I called a few important friends and told them all I couldn't cry, and I never did.

"You're going to have to find a different way to grieve," one of my friends commented.

While I was on the road promoting the memoir, I lost fifteen pounds, and each time it became easier to open the reading of

Butterfly Boy with the phrase, "This book is about my father, who passed away recently."

The next important decision was about the funeral. Since our funds had been depleted, and since my father always said he was not religious so don't bother with a costly service, we opted for cremation. I sent a check to cover most of it. My brother was already outraged at the money pit death was turning out to be: the director of the crematorium had explained to my brother that he would need to purchase a license to keep my father's ashes at home, and another if he expected to transport the ashes across the border. Each permission form came with a $300 price tag, and so, out of anger, my brother informed the director that he was planning on tossing the ashes in the dumpster on his way out. He also brought his own box, but the crematorium director convinced him to purchase a simple no-frills urn because it was more dignified, but without a plaque, because it too came with a fee.

"The urn looked like a cookie box," Alex said. "And just to be on the safe side, as I drove across the border, I shoved the ashes under the passenger seat."

"How's that for irony," I said. "You had to smuggle our father back into México."

"Apá would find that hilarious," Alex said. And then we succumbed to the dead air.

Post Mortem

My father's death certificate told one story:

Cause of death: dilated cardiomyopathy; other significant conditions contributing but not resulting in the underlying cause: Parkinson's, chronic liver disease, acute cholecystitis.

My brother told the following story.

Since he was the only one who could move back and forth across the international border with facility, he made daily trips to the hospital before or after work. Abuela and Amelia didn't drive, so it became difficult to coordinate rides, and he could see how upsetting it was for both of them. Abuela was losing a son. Amelia was losing a husband for the second time.

"I never felt so sorry for a person," he said, describing Amelia's look of defeat.

Over the years, we caught snippets of gossip about the death of her first husband, most of it malicious and coming from our very own relatives in Michoacán because she too had roots in Zacapu. In one version, Amelia was married to an abusive policeman, and when they struggled over a loaded gun, it went off, killing him instantly. She was pregnant with her third son, but they locked her up anyway until the investigation concluded that it had indeed been an unfortunate marital scuffle resulting in an accidental death. In another version, the policeman shot himself while in a drunken rage. Her pregnancy didn't spare her from getting jailed until the investigation cleared her of any wrongdoing. In any case, there was a stigma attached to her reputation. It was my father who took her away from the community of wagging tongues when he met her in Zacapu during one of his visits and brought her back to El Rancho. It was difficult to reconcile Amelia's loud bursts of laughter to this troubling past, so no one brought it up. If I felt any animosity toward her and her children, it was because they came across so happy and carefree, benefiting from my father's choice to be the head of their household and not ours.

"I started lying to them about visiting hours," Alex said. "They were determined to sit there for hours on end, exhausting themselves. The doctors kept sending them home and they wouldn't budge, so they told me not to bring them around as often. It wasn't healthy."

But my brother did stop by as frequently as he could. My father went in and out of consciousness, and when he spoke, he was slightly incoherent and his sentences didn't make any sense. And when he did make sense, it was devastating, asking for forgiveness, calling out for his wives.

"At one point, I had to take him to the bathroom. I had to wipe his ass."

During one difficult afternoon, the doctor came in to check on my father. Alex sat quietly as the doctor studied his patient, but afterward he stood for a moment, staring at my brother.

"You know," the doctor said. "Whoever was taking care of your father was doing a good job. He shouldn't have lasted this long with all those problems he had. And he certainly wasn't taking good care of himself."

"He wouldn't stop drinking," my brother said.

"I can tell," the doctor said. "He was also suffering from depression?"

The question surprised my brother. "I guess so. He had a hard time with the Parkinson's."

"Do you think his depression was so bad that he might have tried to harm himself?"

My brother became uncomfortable with the line of questioning, so he asked the doctor to spit it out. He had been sitting on that chair too long for riddles.

"We found a foreign substance in his system," the doctor said. "Anti-freeze. It's not the kind of fluid a person would imbibe accidentally."

"Is that what's going to kill him?" Alex asked.

"No, his body is what's going to kill him. But that anti-freeze— that complicated matters. And it opens up all kinds of other questions."

"You mean, that someone might have poisoned him?"

The doctor sighed. "No, young man. That he might have tried to poison himself."

When my brother related this conversation to me over the phone, I didn't know what to make of it either. The only silver lining I found was that there was evidence that Amelia loved my father. He had been a father to his stepsons since the oldest was six. He had been a father to his two daughters all their lives. I was sure they loved him back. This man was loved.

"Perhaps it's best to keep that part quiet, Alex," I said. "We don't know what our father was thinking. Clearly he wasn't. And it would be too painful for Amelia, given the history with her first husband."

"But you don't really believe all those stupid stories about her husband, do you?"

"It doesn't matter what you or I believe. It's what our fucked-up relatives want to believe. They'll use this information to hurt her. So let's not give it to them."

"Okay," Alex said.

But we kept coming back to it repeatedly. Had my father attempted to end his suffering? Had he decided he was too much of a burden for his family to deal with? My brother never dared to bring it up the few times our father was lucid.

"Once, he told me to grab his wallet," Alex said. "I dug it out of his pants in the closet. He pulled out his boxing ID."

"Boxing ID?" I said. "From like the 1960s? He carried that around all these years?" It was one of the few images we had of our father at the end of his adolescence, his face clean-shaven and glowing with innocence.

"Yeah. And he gave it to me. Told me that he didn't trust his stepsons to take care of it the way we could."

"We?" I said, seizing on the moment. "As in the two of us? He included me?"

"I assume he did," Alex said.

I became crestfallen. Very selfishly I wanted to be part of something. I had made my choice not to travel all the way to California, but now I was starting to regret it. And when my father slipped into a coma, one that the doctors were certain he wouldn't come out of, I punished myself for my stupidity and walked about aimlessly up and down Manhattan until my brother called to tell me our father had died.

"What was the last thing he said?" I asked. But Alex wouldn't tell me. I needed those last words; I wanted to unpack them into a message I could carry with me for the rest of my journey without him.

"Tell me, tell me," I pleaded with Alex. "I don't care what they were; I just have to know."

"I'm not sure about this," Alex said. "But you have to understand that he was out of it, that he didn't make sense half of the time."

"I got that," I said. "I understand. Now, tell me. What was the last thing he said?"

I stood at the corner of the street. All afternoon, I had been looking for signs and omens. What did it mean to come across a poster of a father standing next to his son? What could I make of that man's tattoo that reminded me of the one my father had on his calf? Should I read something into the moment I came across a bulldozer like the one my father used to drive? What did I know about the man my father became in his forties? In his fifties?

"Turrútut?" I asked again.

"He said, 'I know your brother resents me.'"

Guilt overwhelmed me so completely that I wasn't sure how I made it back to my apartment. My father's last words became branded onto my flesh like a curse. It was then that I realized that all this time I really wasn't looking to forgive my father; I was asking him to forgive me for holding on to this hurt, for blaming him for the wound I kept salting each time I thought about him. What more evidence did I need that he loved me? It was I who had been withholding that affection: the impetuous and stubborn child who never stopped crying about his loneliness as he faced the corner. He was never alone in that room. All he had to do was turn around.

The only thing that still angered me was that my father made orphans of his daughters. The youngest was only eleven, which was the same age Alex was when our mother died. It was a cruel cycle. But my father's death didn't compel me to build a relationship with the second family he had left behind. It didn't seem like an honest thing to do because even though we shared a father, there was no affection between us. The only kind thing I ever did for them was to make sure that my father's house became Amelia's legally. Our nosy relatives stepped in to tell us that our father's house was rightly ours now, and that we could throw those people out whenever we wanted to. But the doctor's words resonated with me: *Whoever was taking care of your father was doing a good job.*

"On that score alone, they earned that house," I said to Alex. And he made sure to draw up the documents in Amelia's name.

"She seemed quite relieved," my brother reported back. "She really did think we were going to kick her out of her house."

My God, I thought to myself. We really know nothing about each other.

And that was the last I heard of Amelia and her family. Once in a while, Alex saw them passing by, but there was very little inter-action between them—maybe a wave or a nod in acknowledgment, if that. Eventually they became neighbors like any others in that growing neighborhood—a unit of strangers swallowed up by other strangers who were just as disinterested and disconnected.

Many years later, I happened to mention to a friend of mine that I had two half sisters whom I had no contact with.

"Have you tried to reach out?" he asked.

"Not really," I said. "I wouldn't even know how."

"Have you tried Facebook?" he suggested.

Since I never used Facebook, it hadn't occurred to me. So out of curiosity I looked them up, expecting to be inundated by a sea of women who happened to share such common Mexican names. But it only took me a matter of minutes to locate their pages. I was stunned by what I saw: My stepmother looked much older, but jovial among her brood; my half sisters were mature young women, having outgrown those girl bodies I called up from memory when-ever I thought about them; and, most surprising of all, there was a picture of my father taken only a few days before his hospitaliza-tion. His body appeared shrunken and worn-out, but the expres-sion on his face betrayed a level of contentment, even peacefulness. I copied the image and sent it to my brother, who became just as devastated by it.

"But you can see it in his face," I insisted. "He was happy. He was a happy man."

I had to say that to feel better about myself. I had to say that to forgive the hurt I had caused.

"I think so, too," Alex said. "I can tell he was happy."

WHEN THE HARD TIMES
BECOME LONELY TIMES

M y brother's marriage to Guadalupe had its problems, but it continued to persevere. He continued his international commute across the border as a gas station manager, and although he was earning dollars, the pay was still low. The household became even more financially strapped after the birth of a second child, André, in 2009. I began to toy with the idea of moving back to the west coast, to be closer to my brother's family, but I had become too attached to NYC and to my solitary lifestyle. I enjoyed the anonymity of the subway rides, the space to think and daydream even while navigating the city crowds. My tiny studio in Queens had become my haven, the only place I felt at peace and finally at home. At least, that's how I explained it to Alex or to anybody who was curious about why I lived so far from my brother when there were only two of us. When I made my annual visit to El Rancho to meet my nephew, to reconnect with my niece, I resisted the tug of sentimentality—the seductive fantasy of family harmony, togetherness, and affection. I yearned for family, but I feared the emotional commitment. It was the same mental block that had kept me single all those years. Just when a romantic relationship began to flourish, I sabotaged it. I felt safer alone.

"And the boyfriend?" Guadalupe would ask each time.

"You mean boyfriends," I replied, and we would start a

naughty banter that kept me from examining the reality of my singlehood.

My brother never asked me about my love life, and I rarely shared any details of it with him, so in effect I didn't have one—I became as asexual as the rest of my family had made me when they finally stopped asking about my plans to get married, and when their questions became exclusively about my line of work and my travels.

I was on the cusp of turning forty when my health began to fail me. I couldn't shake off the dizziness, the fatigue, and the strange feeling that my flesh was weighing me down like an extra coat over my body. I must have lost my balance half a dozen times in public or in the privacy of my apartment before I decided to go to the doctor. Because Parkinson's was the family affliction (besides my father, I knew of one other González male who suffered from it), I was terrified that it too was my fate.

Diagnosis wasn't as conclusive as I had expected. The only treatment I received at first was the use of a cane to keep me from falling, especially because I had stumbled twice on the NYC subway stairs.

"You don't want to break your neck," the doctor said.

The loneliest place in the world is a compromised body. I started using the cane, and immediately my surroundings changed. As did the people around me. Those who pretended not to look at me, out of politeness or otherwise, annoyed me. Those who became overly courteous, offering me assistance, annoyed me even more. My privileges of NYC anonymity had been revoked. Meanwhile, the doctors kept scratching possibilities off their lists: it wasn't fluid in the ear; it wasn't a brain tumor; it wasn't Lyme disease . . . I kept tucked in the back of my mind the recent bout of premature deaths in the family. My two youngest cousins, Daniel and Verónica, had died in their early thirties: one of kidney failure; the other from an aneurysm. It was difficult to get a clear picture of a family medical history because the Gonzálezes didn't go to the doctor and petty family feuds kept them from communicating with each other. When I told this to my own doctors, I felt like I was talking about an ancient warring tribe from another century.

At home, I explained away my use of a cane as a leg injury. Only a few people got the rundown on the medical uncertainty, and most tried to be helpful by referring me to good neurologists. When I wasn't going to work, I stayed home, exhausted of holding my body up with a crutch. But mostly I was tired of the attention and the concern. It was easier to hide out in my apartment. Since I wasn't exercising much anymore, I began to gain weight, which added additional stress to my mobility. If I was somewhat of a recluse before, I was now becoming a shut-in, severing ties with most of the people in my NYC social circle.

When I arrived at El Rancho on the cane, Guadalupe quipped, "Now all you need is a hat to complete the look."

"What look?" I said.

"To look exactly like your father."

"What's up with the cane—you a Rockefeller?" my brother said.

"My leg," I said. And we left it at that.

We left it at that because there were other pressing matters. We had agreed to baptize my nephew, and the ceremony was coming up, so there was a christening outfit to buy, appointments with the priest to contend with, a photographer to book, and a reception to organize. Tío Rafael had been ill for some time and Mari came around more often. And when she did, we understood it was her only means of distraction. She couldn't count on Abuela anymore because Abuela had isolated herself from everyone, and Alex was afraid she wasn't medicating herself correctly.

"She sometimes calls to me and her words don't make sense," Alex said.

It wasn't long before my aunt, my father's only sister, came around to drag Abuela back to California. The dogs were euthanized, the house was gutted, and no one from El Rancho ever saw or heard from Abuela again, until news came around later that summer that she had died.

"When?" I asked my brother when he told me.

"I think about a month ago."

"And you're just now telling me!"

"I'm just now getting the news myself."

I shook my head in disbelief. This was typical González behavior: keep it quiet, withhold as a punitive act. I remembered when Tío Rafael's ex-wife called to tell me that Verónica had died, and the second thing she told me was not to tell Tío Rafael. It seemed like such a cruel request, especially because Verónica was his first-born. So I didn't tell him. I told a cousin who told everyone else. My aunt didn't forgive me for that breach of trust, and so she stopped talking to me as well. I never received the promised invitation to the funeral. But the joke was on her because the silent treatment, the closed door, had always been the González family way.

The following month, Tío Rafael passed away.

"We're dying off," Alex said, and I swallowed hard, hoping that my face would not betray the fear of what for me had now become a possibility.

Despite my body slowing down, my creativity hadn't. I was more productive than I had ever been, publishing up to three books in a single year. I was seized by the notion that I didn't have long to live, that I was the next to go in this string of González family deaths. So I decided to help my brother fulfill one of his dreams — to own a business.

Alex was never shy about admitting how much he hated working at a gas station. It wasn't the labor or the long hours. It was the unpredictable clientele—cranky commuters, nasty tourists, entitled white people, snooty Mexicans. Not to mention the mischief of teenagers making beer runs and stealing off with the merchandise amid fits of laughter, or the more threatening robbers who walked in dog-faced with a loaded weapon. And there were the usual crazies.

"Once this guy walked in and put a sack on the counter and said to me, 'Check this out?'" Alex said. He pantomimed the gesture.

"I thought it was a sack of oranges or something. I thought he was offering me one, so I stuck my hand in, expecting to pull one out." He took a swig of beer to effect a dramatic pause. He had learned this from our father.

"Turns out it was a huge-ass fucking snake, Turrútut. I didn't know if it was alive or dead. All I know is I was expecting to be touching an orange, not no slimy oversized reptile."

"So what did you do?"

"I shit my pants, that's what I did. Right there in the middle of shift. I just wish I had my own little business in El Rancho. Stay close to home. Close to my kids."

Indeed, El Rancho was beginning to thrive with its growing population and paved roads. Long gone were the days of the outhouse and the frequent blackouts. Other enterprising people had set up small food stands along the strip in front of the house, which had once been the irrigation canal. Now it was a busy boulevard. Alex let it slip repeatedly that if he could set up a taco stand, he could see himself eventually leaving the gas station racket with its nutcases and customers who wiped their asses against the bathroom walls.

I too wanted this change for my brother. He didn't ask for money directly, but he convinced me to trust in his dream by showing me the things he could do. He built an outdoor pizza oven and a grill that was the envy of his Facebook buddies with whom he exchanged marinating recipes. When he talked about his vision for promotion and management, he expressed such excitement that it was difficult not to sign on as an investor.

"I'm calling it El Toro Bravo," he said.

Since he had connections with the guys who delivered the beer and sodas to the gas station, he was able to secure patio tables and chairs with the beer logo printed on them. He also commissioned a sign-maker to build a colorful business sign that could be seen from blocks away. El Toro Bravo's pièce de résistance was the illustration of the charging bull with smoke shooting out of its flared nostrils. He bought the taco cart from a man who had become too old to push the contraption around, and Alex turned it into a stationary outdoor kitchen. And as soon as Guadalupe gathered the ingredients for the sauces and prepared the meats, El Toro Bravo was open for business.

"The plan is for Guadalupe to be the cook until I take over eventually," my brother explained. "I'll help out on my nights off."

Guadalupe seemed happy about it. She enjoyed the social atmosphere. And with the kids running around, it was made quite clear that this was a family-friendly establishment.

El Toro Bravo was thriving by 2010 and had quickly become a neighborhood hotspot. It was affordable, the food was tasty, and customers appreciated the humor of its cooks—a young couple whose banter was as spicy as the sauce. I had a chance to see their performance one time, and I was moved by their display of public affection. Whether it was part of the act, it was a convincing show of marital bliss, which set the tone for the rest of the evening.

How could I not become sentimental later that night in bed as I considered how hard-won this moment of happiness had been for Alex, for me? I couldn't help feeling sorry about the absence of both our parents, but here we were, decades later, making do with each other. There were only two of us, and that was fine for now.

When I got back to NYC, I underwent further tests and was presented with the possibility that I might be suffering from multiple sclerosis. I recalled those fundraising telethons from my childhood—muscular dystrophy, Lou Gehrig's disease, cerebral palsy—and I knew I wasn't capable of the strength and dignity of those people who came on stage to bear witness to the challenges and triumphs of living with neurological afflictions. Giving a name to my condition made me spiral into defeat. The more I researched MS, the more I was convinced I suffered from its symptoms, even though I wasn't the typical MS sufferer. That would be young white women, not middle-aged Mexican men. I moved less, drank more, gained the weight that wounded my vanity, and soon I found myself sympathizing with my father, who had drowned his sorrows in the bottle, who escaped into his head in order to avoid facing the reality of the new normal of his Parkinson's disease. And for the first time since my troubled adolescence, I considered suicide.

I didn't want my death to be showy or dramatic. The subway jumper thing was not my style. I went as far as buying a switchblade online, and I imagined myself bleeding out in my bed, surrounded by the many pieces of Mexican art I had accumulated over the years. This haven full of objects from my homeland would make a dazzling tomb. It suddenly struck me that that might be the reason I was attracted to masks and skeletons—their hollow eyeholes upon me no matter where I sat or stood in that tiny apartment. I would die alone, but I would not die without witnesses, and that somehow made my demise less pitiful.

The single detail I couldn't pin down was when. When would I make this graceful exit? At the end of the school year? Between semesters? On some symbolic date, like on the anniversary of my mother's death or of my father's? When I tried to schedule my final day of life, the ridiculousness of the idea made me snap out of it each time. But that was the problem: that there was always a next time.

I withdrew from my social circles more and more. At first, I offered explanations—pressing deadlines, doctor appointments, paper grading—then eventually I didn't bother to respond. I began to drift apart from most of my long-term friendships, ignoring phone calls and text messages until the perfect excuse presented itself to cut ties completely with each and every one of them. When I wasn't teaching class, I would lock myself up in my apartment for days, writing obsessively into the early hours because I was so convinced I had come to the end—whatever I could squeeze out of my creativity would be the last items of my legacy.

When summer arrived and classes were no longer in session, I hid out for even longer stretches of time. I would resurface and see the world marching on as if I didn't matter. Who would miss me anyway? Alex's small business and his marriage were thriving. I had a tangential relationship with his children. When I had my author photo taken, I sent them a framed print. I was satisfied that this was the image they would set on the altar when they remembered me on the Day of the Dead. It was a photograph of my younger, thinner self, before my receding hairline gave me a pronounced forehead, before whatever had seized my body had cursed it to a life of slow suffering. In the evenings, a pain set my back and legs on fire. I would twist into the sheets, smoldering and groaning until I became too tired to remain awake. I woke up a pile of ashes, a remnant of the man I used to be.

Ever the consummate professional, I didn't want to leave any loose ends. I had agreed earlier in the year to attend a summer writers' conference in Montpelier, Vermont, and I refused to cancel. I thought it would be nice to take in the beautiful New England scenery one last time since I was a few weeks away from turning forty. I had decided that dying after my birthday would be most poetic, and I liked the roundness of the figures that would appear thereafter next to my name: 1970–2010.

But a few days into my stay in Vermont, the destructive thoughts that had been swirling in my head subsided. It must have been the sharp green of the leaves or the sky with its blue so pure that it felt like sacrilege to hold on to any negative energy.

The chaos of the city became a distant memory, and I sat on a wooden bench beneath a tree, listening to my own chewing as I ate an apple—the only noise I had to contend with. I still had to use a cane to prop myself up, but even that didn't bother me, not then and there. At that moment, I was happy to be alive. And as I took an afternoon stroll, congratulating myself for reconnecting with life, I received the unexpected call from Guadalupe. My brother had been kidnapped.

"I don't understand," I said. My body was already trembling.

"I'm sure he got kidnapped, I'm sure of it," she said, and the distress in her voice was unsettling. "He was selling his truck and so this man came over to test-drive it with Alex in the passenger seat and they haven't returned."

"How long ago was that?"

"It's been over two hours already," she said. "No one test-drives a truck for that long. And he didn't take his phone because it was supposed to be a quick drive around the block!"

The idea that Alex had been kidnapped was too outlandish to be believed. So I proposed other theories, none of them comforting to either of us. What if there had been an accident? Had she tried calling the hospital?

"I already did and nothing. So I called the police," she said. "And they told me they couldn't do anything until I was certain this was a kidnapping."

"It just doesn't make sense," I said.

This narrative did not belong to someone like Alex. It belonged to politicians and bankers, not to a man who ran a hole-in-the-wall taco stand from his front porch. But I knew that wasn't true. These were desperate times in México. The kidnapping had become the last resort for those who had nothing else to lose. And anyone who did have something to lose—no matter how small—was at risk of losing it. What was the price on my brother's life? I resented all of those clients who sat in his porch assessing his profits, eyeing the truck—not exactly new but not the kind of junket that squealed like a pig as it shifted gears down the boulevard. Any one of these people who savored the food at El Toro Bravo was suspect. As were any of the neighbors. Or passersby. I despised the lot of them.

"Maybe they took the truck and dumped him somewhere," I said and immediately regretted saying that out loud. But picturing him walking back from some strange neighborhood was preferable to imagining him locked in a trunk, or in a windowless cell, or in a tiny ditch with a steel lid—I had no idea where I was getting these ideas, but I couldn't stop them from coming.

"I don't know; I just don't know."

"Well, hang up and stand by the phone," I said after we had exhausted every other possibility. "When they ask for a ransom, tell me. I will pay it. I'll pay anything."

Guadalupe burst into tears, but I couldn't. I had no right, standing so far away, dallying under sunshine and bird song in a place that looked as if the only threat that ever made it here were rain clouds.

I stood paralyzed and lost track of time and began to entertain the idea that this was my punishment for devaluing my own life— the arrogance of my death wish had brought this terrible retribution on me. I made one jittery phone call to a close friend, but just as I was about to explain the anxiety in my voice, my sister-in-law called back. I quickly switched calls.

"What happened?" I said.

"Well, I don't know how to tell you this," she said.

"What? What?"

"He's right here."

After all that emotional turmoil, I wasn't able to grasp any meaning, but neither could Guadalupe communicate, so she put my brother on the line.

"What happened?" I demanded.

"Hey, Turrútut. I'm okay. I'm safe."

"What happened?" I said again.

Everything transpired in a matter of minutes. A man posing as a buyer came to test-drive my brother's truck, but as soon as they made it to the first traffic light, Alex began to suspect something wasn't right. The man was jumpy and refused to acknowledge my brother, who began to make small talk in order to reassure himself that hadn't just let a nutcase get behind the wheel of his truck. Alarmed, Alex asked him to pull over, and that's when the man began to pummel him.

"We started fighting like caged cats. I could see people looking in from the sidewalk, but no one did anything. It was too crazy to be real," Alex said.

"Why didn't you just jump out of the truck?" I said.

"I don't know. I wasn't thinking. All I had in my mind was the idea that this motherfucker was taking something away from my kids. I wasn't going to let him have anything. Not me and not even the truck."

That rage was enough to finally scare the man into stopping the truck and fleeing, leaving Alex hyperventilating and confused. They couldn't have been driving for more than a few minutes, but the surroundings looked unfamiliar, as if he had been sucked through a wormhole and got spat out in a strange land.

"My chest was in pain, and I couldn't breathe. So I drove and drove as far away from that street as I could. And the next thing I knew, I was lost. I didn't have my phone and I didn't even remember my house number, so I kept driving."

Eventually, hours after the ordeal, he began to recognize his whereabouts and headed home.

As soon as he finished the story of his great escape, I yelled out, "You stupid idiot! You got kidnapped in front of your house and you escaped? They know where you live! And about your kids! Why the fuck did you do that?"

"I don't know. I wasn't thinking. I just wanted to be back with my kids, that's all."

New, horrific scenarios began to unfold before me. My brother had seen his kidnapper's face; he wasn't safe. But neither could the police offer any help. This wasn't American detective TV, where precincts kept databases of registered offenders. This was México, where hardship could turn a God-fearing man into fiend. The only way to secure my brother's safety was to relocate his entire household somewhere safe.

Over the years, Guadalupe had talked about wanting to return to her hometown at the tip of the Baja California peninsula. They would have to abandon their taco stand, their house, and most of their belongings, but that was preferable to the dire consequences they could face if they stayed. Their security had been completely compromised in El Rancho. I pulled out everything I had in my bank account and sent it to Alex. A short time later, they loaded whatever could fit in that truck and fled Mexicali. There was no turning back.

"Everything's going to be alright, Turrútut," I said. "It's a new beginning. A new chance at life."

I leaned back in bed at home and breathed, determined to pull myself out of this vortex of depression and self-pity. I had to think about my baby brother. He still needed me.

If I had climbed out of the well of despair, it was only to make room for its next inhabitant. The next two years were rough on Alex. In Guadalupe's hometown, he was the outsider, and making friends outside of his in-laws became a challenge. He had to confront the reality that he would be making Mexican wages at low-level jobs since he had quit his management position at the gas station across the border. That was a shitty job too, but at least it paid in dollars. One of Guadalupe's relatives rented them a small house in the outskirts of town, and what had started out being a cozy three-bedroom rental was quickly turning into a crowded, suffocating space now that the kids were growing up and taking up more room.

The only saving grace for Alex was the town's proximity to the water. It was a fishing village and one of Jacques Cousteau's favorite ecological hotspots along the Sea of Cortez. Tourist season brought him seasonal opportunities because he was fluently bilingual, and he also got to join the excursions on fishing boats.

"That's heaven for me, Turrútut," he said. "You just can't get that kind of fishing on the shore. You have to go far into the sea, away from all the problems on land."

Those tourist guide gigs were easy and enjoyable, but they didn't pay well, and that began to affect the harmony of his marriage. To help him out, I began to send him money whenever he requested it, but the requests were coming so often that I negotiated an allowance in order to keep from draining my bank account.

Whenever we spoke on the phone, I kept hearing such sadness in his voice. He felt like a failure, unable to provide for his own children. His in-laws began to question his effectiveness as head of a household. He spoke longingly about his grill, his spacious house in El Rancho, his little taco stand—a dream that had been dashed only a few short months after it had become a reality. All of this must have contributed to the health issues he began to endure: high blood pressure, hypertension, sleep disorders, fatigue—the list was long and alarming. The doctor's recommendation that he rest seemed like the most ridiculous treatment at a time when he needed the money, when he needed to prove to his in-laws, to his family, and to himself that he was a man.

"But you *are* a man, Alex, you're a *good* man," I said to him. I was still working out my own health issues, so I didn't even bother to bring them up.

"I wish we had never left Mexicali," he said.

That made me feel complicit in his misery, maybe even

responsible for it. But I had to remind us both that if he had stayed, he might have ended up dead.

"Maybe it would be better that way," he said.

My mouth went dry. The gravity of those words, even if impulsively stated, brought back the uncomfortable legacy of self-destruction that I was beginning to suspect was also the González way. We were a family of silent suffering, of hiding in the shadows in shame. Where had we learned this behavior? Or was it simply woven into our genes? I wanted to reprimand my brother, or at the very least offer words of consolation and encouragement, but that would have been the most hypocritical of acts from the person who pushed his circle of confidantes away because words were as brittle as leaves breaking apart in the wind when confronting something as overpowering as depression.

I didn't say anything. I pretended I hadn't heard him say such a painful thing. It made hanging up the phone after our conversation much easier. It made it possible to lie down a country away and then rise the next morning without having to succumb to the guilt.

My response to my brother's cry for help was to send more money. That is all I could spare from so far away, and I began to wonder if this had been my strategy all along—to distance myself from my family in order to stay clear of their crises, in order to pull out this handy excuse for my absence from their hospitalizations, their funerals, their terrible days.

The money paid bills, purchased clothes and nourishment, but it did little to temper the tension between my brother and his wife. It also paid for the medications, but it didn't cure Alex's health problems, which seemed more like symptoms of his emotional distress.

"The only thing the doctor tells me is to rest," Alex complained. "Who the fuck has time to rest?"

"Does he mean rest your body or rest your mind?" I said.

"What? What are you talking about?"

I hesitated to elaborate. I recalled the many times close friends suggested therapy and I scoffed at the idea. I knew what to expect from my brother—we were of the same blood.

"You know, maybe talk to someone."

"Like counseling? With a shrink?" He sounded incredulous.

"Yes," I said softly.

"Turrútut, that's white people ideas. White people do therapy."

That's right, I thought. And the Gonzálezes turn to the bottle. They drain their will to live in the tiny quiet corners of the house.

"You wouldn't consider it?" I said.

"No," he said. Then he added, "I don't know. Maybe."

But he didn't. And neither did I. Instead, we continued on our journeys, bearing the pangs of stress, isolation, and sadness.

GREETINGS FROM NEW YORK CITY, 1968

My brother's question was innocent enough, a conversation-starter fired off during our weekly international phone call—he still in Baja California Sur, me sticking to New York—three hours apart, sometimes four, depending on the time of the year. He might have thought it was a unique way to begin, a different starting point other than *What's up, Turrútut?* I dialed and he answered, and as soon as I said, "Hey, it's me," Alex said, "Turrútut, did you ever see that photograph of our father in New York City?"

I spun the Rolodex of memory, of all those tales, exaggerated or invented, that Apá used to hook people's attention with. When I was six and my brother was five, it worked like a charm, like the time he came home bloodied, his lip and thumb sliced open, his clothes disheveled, claiming he had jumped over the cemetery wall to take a piss and then had to fight off the mummies. My brother and I sat transfixed by his courage, the back kick he still had strength to show us even though it was late and our mother stood at the doorway shaking her head in disapproval. At the time, I didn't know what that look on her face meant, until I saw it many times later during his moments of drunkenness. Apá's energy for telling a story never waned, and he wasn't ruffled by expressions of disbelief or if members of his audience lost interest—as long as there was one person listening, that was enough to keep him going. Sadly, I was usually not that person because I had stayed away, which is why my Rolodex started coming up empty, its lack of reference evidence of my distance from my father during my adolescence and beyond.

Though if Apá had ever been to NYC, I would have latched on to that tidbit, if not at the moment of the first telling then definitely after NYC became part of my everyday reality. Certainly I wouldn't have wanted to regale my family with details of my new home in the Big Apple as if none of them had ever been there. The very idea of Apá in NYC seemed outrageous.

"I don't believe it," I said to my brother.

I was ready to offer by way of a rebuttal the time I was visiting El Rancho and the three of us sat watching the news on Mexican television. At one point, there was a snippet of footage of Columbus Circle, the huge statues on the corner of Central Park with its infestation of pigeons. I said to them, "Look! That's New York, that's where I live!" And Apá had quipped, "And those pigeons . . . are they edible?" That was just one of many opportunities my father had to tell that he had been there, but he never did. He didn't offer that story about his trip to NYC, I concluded, because he didn't have it.

"For real," Alex said. "It's a photograph of our father standing over a little stove in a tiny kitchen. I saw it in Abuela's photo album, but she didn't know where it was taken. So later, when I asked him, he said that it was a picture of him making breakfast before looking for a job in New York. He was living in the Bronx at the time."

Stunned, I didn't respond. I couldn't imagine Apá even knowing about places like the Bronx.

"Are you there?" my brother said.

"Is that all he said?" I asked.

"That's it. And then he started talking about other things, so then I forgot about it until it suddenly popped up in my head this morning."

I became overwhelmed by the pang of loss. There was no way to find out more because Apá had been dead for years now, and so had Abuela. Her albums, likely the property of some relative we didn't speak to, were no longer available to either of us.

"Wow," I said. "Well, that knocked the wind out of me. Are you sure he didn't just make that up?"

My brother laughed. "I guess we'll never know."

"That just isn't fair," I said, and though I was referring to the never-knowing, I was also thinking about how my access to Alex was also limited. We were relegated to being two voices in different countries, holding on by a telephone wire, and even then I was only metaphorically speaking since all I had was a cell phone. Good grief; I wasn't attached to anything. Not even to my fucking wall.

So I latched on to the history of this photograph that was real enough though the story behind the image seemed questionable. Wasn't it always that way with my father? If I were a more cynical son, I would call it fiction. But this wasn't about me; it was about my father the storyteller, the entertainer, he who could embellish a late-night walk from a drunken brawl at a bar into a battle with the undead.

If there was any truth to that photograph linking my father to the Bronx, then it must have been taken circa 1968, shortly after my father turned twenty-one, thinking himself a man because he had grown an attractive mustache, so he went seeking out both adventure and employment in the United States. I had grown up situating my family's second migration in the early 1960s exclusively to California since this was familiar territory. Abuelo had been born in Riverside, south of LA, during the first migration back in the 1930s, and I was born in Bakersfield, north of LA, in 1970 on my mother's first journey north. The vertical paths from Michoacán to California did not appear to vary through the generations. So the possibility of my father wandering to the east coast opened up a startling narrative about who he was as a bachelor, just two years away from eloping with his girlfriend, who had become pregnant with me.

My father's early adulthood is the one fuzzy period in the family lore. Over the years, I had heard from his siblings many stories about his childhood antics in Michoacán—how Tío Rafael once led him around with a string around his neck because that's what was done with the beetles that were as dark as my father; how Tío Rafael used a homemade bow and arrow to knock my father out of a tree, and the scar on my father's waist had swollen into a mole; how Tía Melania and my father, neither of them older than ten, were trying to figure out a gas oven and she stood back and watched him singe his eyebrows and eyelashes. Apá offered plenty of comic relief for the family in those days. Later, I realized that they held on to the funny moments because the somber ones were too painful to revisit as often—about Abuela losing two infant daughters; about the times she sent her children to scour the back of the town market for discarded but still edible fruit and vegetables; about the hours she spent cutting garnish for the butchers, who always decorated their goods in those days with sprigs of cilantro, chopped onion, and teeth of garlic that shimmered like pearls next to the red meat; about the nights of unyielding abuse from a frustrated, angry Abuelo.

Abuelo as a father held the key to a likely reason Apá left or fled or escaped to the other coast back in 1968. I had done the same in 1998, when the thought of living close to my family filled me with anxiety because I couldn't reconcile my college years as an out gay youth with my family's don't-ask-don't-tell policy. So instead of going west after I dropped out of a PhD program at the University of New Mexico, I headed east, to NYC.

I imagined Apá's expectations as a young man were no different from my own: an opportunity to define himself apart from those he loved but who troubled him. He and I were both first-born males, the burden of leadership and responsibility was upon us, but so too the privileges of whims and impulses, like leaving home and coming back when we felt like it—the right to play the archetypal prodigal son.

Abuelo was a bully and a brute, but what my brother and I endured the many years we lived with him did not compare to what his own sons had to contend with back in the day. Apá and Tío Rafael reminded us of this fact whenever my brother or I had cause to complain about how Abuelo wouldn't let us use the telephone or locked us out of the house if we stayed out after that cruel seven o'clock curfew. These oppressions didn't even come close to the regulations *they* were subjected to.

"Remember the chickens, you?" Tío Rafael said to my father, who nodded calmly as he sipped his beer. "Your grandfather insisted the damn things sleep on their perches. So every evening we had to frighten them up to the nests so that they wouldn't lay their eggs on the ground. It was the most ridiculous demand."

They laughed at the memory of it, but I didn't find it amusing. They preferred to retell these strange flashes from the past because they refused to talk about the more serious matters, like the beatings they got and the beatings my brother and I got. And then my head swelled with rage because I knew he also beat Abuela. He would beat her in the dark, and I could hear her holding back her cries. He hit her because he couldn't beat his grown-up sons anymore or his adolescent grandsons. My father and uncle knew this as well, but none of us spoke up about it. No one did anything to protect Abuela. What happened out of sight was never real enough to confront in the spaces we shared, like the living room, where Abuelo sat comfortably next to Abuela, the two of them laughing at the antics of the Mexican comics on the television. They seemed so compatibly matched, and so it seemed vulgar to even hint at the knowledge of what transpired in their bedroom in the cover of dark.

As a young man, my father had ambitions other than dedicating his life to harvesting the crops of southern California. At one time, he wanted to become a boxer and had trained in his hometown of Zacapu, where young athletes were either long-legged cyclists or stocky pugilists. My father at five foot two was shaped like a bull, all chest and calves. He must have had some talent since it warranted the purchase of red training gloves and a red pair of silk trunks that he hauled with him years after he gave up on that dream. I would later hear that he wasn't a very good boxer at all, especially from my mother's sisters, who liked to tease him about it in front of me. I remember feeling sad for him during these jabs because I knew that his boxing days were special to him and that it hurt him to have them disparaged so callously.

Only once do I recall him bringing up the subject when Alex and I stumbled into him Sunday afternoon at home, the only time he claimed time in front of the television because the station featured boxing. We knew not to disturb him, so we sat quietly on the couch at his side, biding our time to take over the television.

During a commercial break, he announced, "That could have been me."

It was then that I realized how vague those boxing days were, which seemed odd for a man who could improvise as seamlessly as if he were tying his shoes. At the same time, I took pleasure in the fact that maybe my father *was* capable of keeping something to himself, the way I did about the crushes I had on other boys. If my father had a private joy like me, then that endeared me to him a little more.

"Why did you stop?" I dared to ask. In the back of my mind, I remembered my aunts' teasing, and suddenly I felt insensitive about the question, but it was too late to take it back. My father didn't respond. He simply grinned and tilted his head to the side to indicate he had no answer, that this was one of those rare moments he was going to remain quiet.

So instead he suggested, "Maybe one of you will become a boxer."

The statement made me nervous. But I had no reason to fret. When I became a teenager, my father had given up on the idea of me becoming a boxer because I had bad eyesight and swung a hook like a girl. Alex became the athlete, though he chose football as his sport, to my father's disappointment because he had found a gym in the area that trained young men to box.

That grin, however, stayed with me. I collected them over the years, like that time my mother finally confronted him about his drinking, the time he had to come pick up Alex and me in Michoacán after our mother had died, and the time Abuela gave him money to bail him out of financial woes when his second marriage was hurting. The grin was his response to a deep pain or loss.

If my father left home at the age of twenty-one, it had to have been after an argument with Abuelo. Over money, over freedom, over a girlfriend—over a punishment he deemed unjust. Abuelo was always asserting control over his sons' affairs. I pictured my father as a rebellious young man finally reaching the breaking point, mustering the courage to gather his few belongings in a duffle bag and set out on foot. His greatest heartache must have been leaving his little brother, Rafael, behind—they had never been apart. The family was living in either southern California or central California, but what's certain is that they were toiling the grape fields, that their clothes smelled of sulfur and their skins were still warm from absorbing hours of summer heat.

I saw my father arrive at the station. Maybe his plan was to head south, back to Michoacán, where dozens of doors would open for him without question. He was Rigoberto—the joyful one, the jokester, the happy drunk. He was always the highlight of the party. But maybe, for those same reasons, he decided not to return to the familiar and the comfortable—not if he wanted to take ownership of his story. I'm not sure how much a bus ticket across the country cost in those days, but my father would not have been able to afford it had Abuela not discreetly shoved some money in his pocket when he said his good-byes. He might not have told his father he was leaving, but he was always kind to his mother, and so he let her in on his decision, maybe the night before, after the big fight that ended with Abuelo telling my father to leave if he didn't like it and with my father saying that he didn't like and so he was going to leave.

Why NYC? Maybe he had seen something on television that appealed to him: the rivers of energy because everyone had direction and function, or the excitement of a nightlight with pretty girls in red heels and bars that kept their doors opened for anyone, or the wide streets lined with buildings taller than cathedrals— they had to be in order to answer all those prayers that walked into the city from every corner of the world—and he was determined to be the newest member of the congregation. Or maybe he simply chose at random, an impulsive selection made according to the schedule of departures: "Next bus to New York City departing in ten minutes!" And ten minutes later he was on the road.

But since he claimed to have been cooking breakfast for friends, it was more likely he had reconnected with other young men who had already made that journey east, who told him, "Hey, what the fuck are you doing wasting away in the fields like a cross-eyed donkey? The city is where it's at. Come over!" And so he did.

The drive across country took days, long enough for him to reflect on what it meant to have left his family. With each mile, the gravity of the fight, the size of his oppressions, became smaller and smaller, so he began to second-guess his decision, though not enough to turn back because no matter how far away he journeyed, the sting of Abuelo's ultimatum never disappeared completely. If ever there was a way to prove to his father that he wasn't a child anymore, it was like this—surviving the outside world alone with only his balls and his gut to guide him.

He was a social creature. Solitude was not his thing. So he struck up conversations with the other passengers around him, and soon a nostalgic mood seized the travelers because no one was going home to NYC; home was back there—California, or the border, or Coahuila, or D.F., or Michoacán. New York was only the next stop. Not the last one. If the bus was full of Mexicans, then it was certain that as they journeyed farther away from home, the more tenaciously they held on to the names of their hometowns, to the foods they missed, and so they called them out in their storytelling punctuated with laughter, pausing only to sigh. Like this, my father learned his first valuable lesson: these were the precious stones immigrants carried in their pockets. They would make separation tolerable and remind them to stay alive in order to make their way back. His own stones were getting heavy, but that was the price paid for leaving. No complaining. On a journey with so much uncertainty ahead, this might end up being the smallest of the burdens.

What was the Port Authority Bus Terminal like in the late 1960s? My father must have felt his heart fluttering with excitement and anxiety as he joined the crowds of strangers whose voices spoke in unrecognizable languages. The volition was all-consuming; the speed, stress-inducing. Everyone walked with purpose, and so he tried to make himself fit in somehow. The bus station was nothing like the smaller versions he had come across in Morelia or even Guadalajara. This beast was all mouth and gnashing teeth, a slippery tongue of a floor that swallowed people whole as it spat others out. Unfettered, he stood up straight and marched right out into the street as if he knew where he was headed. Maybe his friends were waiting for him in a nearby deli and they introduced him to the delicacies of the region—lox and bagels, roast beef sandwich, the pizza slice that folded into an envelope so that he could eat it while walking. But more likely they gave him an address. Not in the Bronx but in Manhattan because that's where they all worked. They told him to wait on a bench in a park nearby until quitting time. It was easier that way.

But it was hours until quitting time, and my father was not one to sit around and people-watch. So he squeezed his duffle bag beneath his arm and went for a stroll. The city was a grid. There was no getting lost. He took in the dirty chaos of Times Square, the elegant entrances of hotels and theaters, the formality of doormen, the mischief of young boys who navigated the sidewalks so confidently because they had been born in this city though their parents were born in Ireland, Italy, Cuba, and Puerto Rico. He would have to wait to ride the subways, but what a thrilling prospect—how bodies descended and ascended the stairs with efficiency. This was a city in constant motion. Even the marquees did not look stationary as they flashed and dazzled like cabaret dancers. Could he see himself staying here? It was too soon to tell. The only thing he was sure of in that moment was that he had become part of the city's circulation the minute he stepped off that bus.

When he finally met up with his friends, they were unrecognizable in their fatigue, their faces wilted at the end of the workday, and for a moment he second-guessed his decision because these were the same faces he saw in the fields. So what was different except that in the city they went home and were still not home? But he shook that question out of his head. It was too soon to sully his arrival with negative thought.

The long subway ride to the Bronx was oddly soothing, and people in the car exchanged places with people on the platform at every stop. He would have to memorize the underground map and learn to understand the conductor's announcements in that nasally New York accent since he was barely literate and didn't trust his skill for quickly reading signs. On the way, his friends still took the time to ask about his family, about news from home—it was polite chatter, not the usual banter that's the public exchange of young men since they were very tired, their eyes glassy and small because they were minutes away from falling asleep but still a dozen stops away from their neighborhood.

Twelve stops later, they exited the subway. After a short walk through an alley and getting startled by a barking dog, which provided the only moment of levity, his friends unlocked the door and welcomed him into his temporary home. It was a bachelor space, no doubt about that. It smelled of sweaty feet and the masculine musk of bodies that clocked in an additional two or three hours of perspiration on a commute after a twelve-hour shift. The only splash of color was a poster of la Virgen de Guadalupe, a Mexican flag, and a delicate red vase from Chinatown that one of the young men planned to take back to his mother for the holidays. A black suitcase against the wall was doubling as a shelf, and a white stuffed bear with a pink ribbon around its neck looked so out of place among the contents of that room that was empty of femininity and childhood.

The first night was painful. Not only did the remorse of his disrespect against his father set in, but he longed for the company of his little brother—his dirty riddles, his childish notion that wearing two shirts made his body look bigger, that wearing sunglasses made him look older—and he longed to hear his mother's laugh. How he missed Amá, the Purepecha woman who didn't know how to read or write, except for her signature—a simple scribble in all lowercase letters that endorsed her check from the fields every other week. She must have lost her sleep and was likely up at this hour watching the curtains catch moonlight and hoping her prayers, which were only whispers in bed, were loud enough for God. How bad he felt that he couldn't keep his eyes open. How unfair that he didn't have any trouble falling asleep. But this was the sacrifice of worried mothers: they stayed awake to watch over their errant sons.

The next morning, the movement of bodies woke him up, and his friends apologized but it was a workday, so piercing lights went on and so did the radio because it kept them from dozing off again. My father, to express his gratitude, got up and squeezed into the tiny kitchen. *He would* be making breakfast today and maybe the day after, until he found a job and became just another one of the guys, not the unemployed one who could sleep in and wander around as he looked for work.

Maybe the gesture was deeply appreciated, or maybe no one had the energy to give more than a low-voiced thank you, but one of them thought it was a noteworthy occasion—Rigoberto's first day in the Bronx. He grabbed his camera and snapped a black-and-white shot of my father shirtless over the stove, one hand on the skillet and the other stirring the spatula—I remembered it now; I was certain of its existence.

Though Apá never spoke to me about it, he *did* walk through the streets of NYC before I did, and in doing so, he had paved a path for me. When I arrived thirty years later in 1998, I had only followed in my father's footsteps. Perhaps he never told me because he sensed how proud I was that I had achieved something all on my own—independence in a place no González had ever been. It was my personal triumph, my claim to a territory where I would write my singular narrative as the hero of the story. Wasn't this the way to manhood? What a bubble burst it could have been had my father said, "Yes, New York City, of course, I've been there, done that." So he opted to keep that little part of his personal history to himself. Besides, no one remembered it. No one knew how long he had stayed or why he came back.

The real mystery was why Alex didn't remember that photograph while I was visiting from NYC and our father was still alive. How did it vanish from his memory all these years, only to reappear like some biblical miracle to deliver a message from the other side? And was I reading that lesson correctly? Unlike my father, I never returned. Unlike my father, I didn't wake up one morning, rattled by the sounds of sirens and street traffic, and decide that this wasn't where I belonged. How he must have been eager to save his earnings, how he must have skipped a few nights out with the guys in order to buy his little brother a pair of sunglasses and his mother one of those red vases from Chinatown. And then one evening, the pull of those stones in his pocket became too much. The others did not object. They had seen this before. They knew who had it in them to endure the isolation and who was going to crack after a week or a month. They were fine saying good-bye because there was always another man ready to take over for the one who left.

Apá turned in his key without ceremony and made his way to the bus station alone, carrying the same duffle bag he arrived with. What a relief he must have felt when the bus finally squeezed out of the Manhattan bustle and made its way through the open roads of Pennsylvania where the sky was clear and the clouds appeared to breathe. Besides the stones in his pocket, he also had a small wad of cash to prove to his father that he could earn a living on his own, though he didn't want to. On his own, that is. On that score, his father was right: one suffered apart from family. But time and distance heals all wounds. And money, my father added as he scratched the bills he had stuffed into his sock. He couldn't help but let out a laugh thinking that he had to buy his way back into the family nest. Abuelo wouldn't have it any other way. His laughter caught the attention of the man across the aisle.

"Going home, son?" the man asked.

My father smiled and said, "Yes, sir, I certainly am." And the phrase pirouetted in the air because it also said he knew where he was meant to be. Life was hard with family but life was harder without it. How fortunate he was to learn the difference. His place was among his loved ones and—father, forgive me; mother, receive me; brother, stay near me—I'll never ever ever leave again.

BROTHERLY LOVE

Summer 2014. My mobility had improved under the care of a new doctor. The formula was actually quite simple: rest, diet, and exercise. But simple formulas were the easiest to neglect, particularly as an academic. Meetings took precedence over meals, grading and class preparation ate up my sleep time, and the commute to the university stressed my body, especially when no one on the crowded subway trains offered me a seat even though I struggled to maintain my balance while leaning on a cane. But as soon as summer arrived, I stayed close to home, taking early morning walks and regulating my eating and sleeping schedules. By now, I had distanced myself from most of my acquaintances, so I had all the permission I needed to hide out and focus on my writing, which was the only pleasure I had left. Writing allowed me to vacate this body and its inconvenient limitations. Sometimes, I became so consternated when I woke up to the reality of my weaknesses that I scrambled to the computer in order to flee all over again.

Yet somehow I managed to start a new relationship. I had given up on the notion of dating, let alone becoming intimate with anyone, because I couldn't imagine anyone being attracted to a man on a cane, whose disability became more prominent than this age or ethnicity. I still experienced desire, but it remained an unreachable horizon since I lost the nerve to flirt, afraid that if anyone flirted back, it was a response fueled by sympathy. The last thing I wanted was a pity fuck.

I had seen Roger a few times before during my morning walk when the same group of commuters passed me on the sidewalk to catch the train. I stayed close to the wall and out of the way. Perhaps it was the look of approval I gave each time I saw him in his starched white shirt and solid-colored tie that finally prompted Roger to say hello. I almost tumbled into the wall, caught off guard by the attention.

"Easy there, buddy, you all right?" he said. He stopped to place his hand on my shoulder.

"Sorry," I said. "I'm fine, thank you."

"Don't apologize," he said. "I've seen you out here every day this week. You doing some kind of therapy for an injury?"

"Right. A leg injury."

"Well, keep it up," he said before rushing off. "You're looking better and better each time." He winked.

Flattered after getting noticed by a younger man, I made sure to stick to the same schedule and to say good morning to Roger a few more times before I dared ask him to meet up for coffee. And then it was dinner. And eventually we took turns sleeping over at each other's apartments.

Roger's affection offered me a different kind of solace. Nude, we shared our physical imperfections and didn't mind them. He was ten years younger, but he confessed that he had a huge insecurity about his weight. Faced with such honesty, I decided to come clean about the cane. I admitted to him that I had lied about the leg injury, that I was battling an illness.

"I might end up in a wheelchair someday," I said.

After an uncomfortable pause, Roger leaned over and kissed me. "We'll cross that bridge when we get there," he said. I was so moved by his response that I promised I wouldn't deny him anything. That was my first mistake.

Brotherly Love

My brother, on the other hand, was still dealing with the stress of a troubled marriage, with the feelings of failure that came from being unable to hold onto a job because the stiffness in his elbows and knuckles was making it impossible to perform even the simplest of tasks.

"I can't even fucking sweep, Turrútut, or lift a crate of bread."

"But I told you, Alex, to rest. I can send you more money. Don't worry about that," I pleaded.

"You don't understand," he said. "I don't want people to see me not working. It's a different world down here—a man who lets his wife do all the labor is no man at all. I see her family judging me whenever they see me. I see Guadalupe judging me each time she comes home from her job. I don't think she loves me anymore."

"Don't be ridiculous, Alex; of course she loves you. You have two children together and together you built a home."

"And what kind of a home is a home without a man?"

I finally understood the role of parents in the grown-up stage of a person's life. I finally understood how we had been cheated out of a valuable resource because we had no mother to console us during our heartbreaks and no father to counsel us during our headaches. As his gay older brother with a long history of failed relationships, I had very little to offer Alex. We had traveled very different paths toward adulthood. He was married and had children; I was single. He had returned to México; I had fled to New York. His paradise was sailing out into the open sea; mine was to sink into the whirlpool of the computer screen. I had been depending on that escape more lately because my relationship with Roger was beginning to strain.

Maybe it had been there from the beginning, but my gratitude had kept me blind. Or rather, I allowed it to happen because it was a relief to have someone else take control during a time I felt I had lost control over my ailing body. Roger made every decision in the relationship: he decided when we should see each other, when to have sex, what to eat, where to meet, where to go, what to do. The few times I made alternate suggestions or even dared to protest, Roger snapped at me, threatening to cancel our plans altogether. Afraid of upsetting him further, I relented. What began as casual requests (shave your face if you want me to kiss you, don't wear earrings when we go out, wear boxer briefs, you look better in boxer briefs) became deal-breakers that sent him reeling into fits of anger because I had ruined the mood. Once, we met up in his apartment, and he became annoyed because I had bought the wrong brand of cranberry juice for his Cape Cods.

Frustrated, I blurted out, "What's the big fucking deal, Roger?"

"The big fucking deal is that you don't follow directions," he said.

"Directions? Am I not housebroken enough for you? Are you going to discipline me like an animal too?"

"That's a great idea," he said. So he grabbed my cane and threw it out into the hallway. "Go fetch!"

A light went out inside of me, and I couldn't react. Instead, I crawled along the furniture and walls to retrieve my cane. The sight of my jittery movements must have softened Roger's disposition because he pleaded for forgiveness. But I had come across men like Roger before. I didn't know what was more pathetic: that I had allowed myself to become involved with an abusive man again, or that I knew that even this display of humiliation wasn't enough to convince me to leave him.

If my brother shared the most private details of his marital problems, I didn't reciprocate by telling him about Roger. Roger had become increasingly more selfish in bed, content with satisfying himself and pushing me away when he decided the moment of intimacy was over. He would ask me to come over, and halfway to his apartment, I would get a text that something had come up, that he couldn't see me after all, and I would walk back home and wait for an apology or an explanation, but neither ever came. I was afraid to let go of Roger because I knew I would need a shoulder to cry on. I sensed something dramatic coming my way because my weekly conversations with my brother were becoming more and more distressing. I proposed once again that he see a counselor, but he rebuffed my suggestion—that was not what he was about.

"Well, do you have a friend you can talk to at least?" I said.

"I don't have those kinds of friends here," he said. "I only have you."

What a sad prospect, I thought to myself, that my brother's only hope is a man who lets his lover mistreat him because it's the only love he thinks he can get. We were both fucked.

I thought of making a trip down to Baja California Sur to see my brother, to offer him an embrace, but my body couldn't handle travel anymore. I had begun to turn down professional offers to read or lecture in other parts of the country, which cut into my annual income, and each month I had to scramble to meet my brother's financial needs. So I did my best the only way I knew how, the only thing I could do confined to my apartment: I wrote. I wrote essays, interviews, book reviews, highlighting other writers, escaping into their words. The momentary haven of their imaginations was more rewarding than the paltry payments, but eventually the money added up to a remittance. Meanwhile, I was juggling a full-time university teaching job, a few online courses, and a ghostwriting gig—these last two were freelancing opportunities I had once scoffed at, but I set aside my arrogance and snobbery for the extra income. Rising every day at 4:00 a.m. to sit in front of the computer to work on someone else's drab life story was draining the pleasure out of writing. I began to resent my weak body, my brother, the stale tasks I had seized on to earn money. By the end of the year, I had not replenished my savings and, wallowing in despair, spent what little I had on alcohol.

Inevitably, that phone call I was dreading came. I was on my couch at home, looking over a student's thesis. Roger had not contacted me in over a week, and I was fine with that for the time being. We had been seeing each other for less than a year, but during the last month, our dates had become more and more sporadic.

"Hey, Alex," I said when I answered the phone. It didn't dawn on me that it was usually me who dialed him in order to deal with the expense of the international call.

"I'm so depressed," he said. "I think I'm going to kill myself."

My body slumped over on the couch and I dropped the phone. I had no clue what had just happened to my body—I was conscious, so I hadn't fainted. But I couldn't worry about that; I had to talk my brother through this. I didn't hang up until I was satisfied that he wasn't going to harm himself or anyone else around him. The frightening headlines that announced domestic tragedies flashed in my head, so I resorted to the most desperate of measures— I told my brother a horrible truth.

"If you kill yourself, Alex, you might as well take me with you. Because I am not going to be left alone in this world."

Though I kept myself composed during the conversation, as soon as we ended the call, I began to shiver. I texted Roger, and to my surprise, he agreed to let me come over.

"Oh, Roger," I said as soon as he opened his door. I wanted to throw myself into his arms, but he stepped back.

"What is this?" he said.

"What is what? I need you right now. I need you to be here for me. I just finished talking to my brother and—"

"Look, no offense, but I didn't sign up to listen to your family problems. We can hang out, we can fuck, but I'm zero percent here for drama."

I sighed. I tried to push back inside me all the grief I had been prepared to share with Roger, but it was too much, too devastating. Numb, I sat down on his couch and stared at the blank television screen.

"And if you're going to sit there like a paraplegic, you might as well do that at home," Roger said. "Not having it."

I turned to face him. "Why would you use that word?" I said.

"What word?"

"Paraplegic. Why do you have to be so cruel about my disability?"

"I don't understand you people. You want to be treated just like everybody else, but then you're all touchy about little things like words."

My eyes narrowed. I suddenly saw Roger as far away as he had kept himself all along. Whatever had anchored me to his conditional affection had begun to lose its hold.

"You're not going to start crying, are you?"

I had the urge to knock him down with my cane, or to do some disarray to his beloved orderly place. His apartment was as clean and uncluttered as a showroom, and it bothered him once when I moved one of the coasters on the coffee table closer to where I was sitting. "Why don't you move closer to the coaster?" he had suggested. But I didn't want to go that route. I was a man in my forties; I should know better.

"Listen, Roger," I said. "I'm sorry I wasted your time."

"That's fine," he said. "Just don't do it again."

"Let me finish," I said.

His eyes widened.

"But I'm even sorrier that I wasted mine." I picked myself up and headed for the door.

"You walk out on me now, that's forever," he said.

"God, I certainly hope so."

I knew as soon as I said it that it was one back talk too many. And maybe that's why I said it, because I wanted what was about to come next to take place. Otherwise I wouldn't reach the moment of reckoning. Roger pushed his fist into my body and knocked me off balance. My face struck the door, and then I slid down to the floor.

"You see—"

I looked up at him and finished his sentence. "—what I made you do?"

He remained silent and expressionless as I picked myself up and started to exit his apartment. Just as I was about to shut the door behind me, I heard him mumble something in that remorseful tone he liked to use whenever he hurt me, but I didn't even feel the urge to disrupt the momentum. Whatever he said would have to stay inside with him. And I would keep myself out.

A calm came over me when I got to the main boulevard and joined the flow of pedestrians on the sidewalk, everyone going about their business, each person walking with purpose. How good to have a direction and a destination. How comforting to know that every step forward made a memory of the previous step.

I called my brother the next day to check on his emotional state. I called him the day after that and the day after that. And after each phone call, I had to drink a few martinis in order to cope with the stress of trying to remain calm while he voiced the most frightening thoughts. I had to keep it together in order to call him the next day. I had to keep it together in order to maintain the semblance of composure as I commuted to work to teach class and sat patiently through meetings while my head spun. Was it my brother or was it the alcohol? Maybe it was both. Meanwhile, I could feel my body declining because I began to neglect my diet and exercise. The weight gain aggravated my joints because of the extra pressure I placed on the cane. My doctor wasn't pleased.

"You're adding to your list of complications, my friend," he said. "Your blood pressure is up; your cholesterol is up. You're looking at a dire future if you don't lose some weight."

"And lose weight how?" I snapped. "I can barely move."

"Weight loss is mostly about what you eat," the doctor said. "And what you drink." He raised his eyebrows by way of indictment, and I blushed.

Since my brother and I communicated exclusively by phone, he wasn't seeing the negative changes in my body, and neither was I seeing them in his. But our voices betrayed our anxieties—the long pauses, the distracted conversations, the exchanges that were now stripped of banter or memory triggers. *Do you remember?* we used to ask each other, just like my father used to do when he wanted to set journey into motion. But we weren't going anywhere anymore. Phone call after phone call, we were stuck in the same dark corner.

"Maybe Guadalupe and I should split up," he proposed one time. "Just for a little while."

And I thought how unfortunate that our parents weren't around to offer him refuge, and that I was so far away, it was impractical, since he wanted to stay close to his kids.

"Maybe that will help," I said. "Don't worry about the money. I can take care of that."

I swallowed hard because it wasn't that easy anymore. I had continued to pile up the freelancing work, which had become physically demanding as I hunched over the computer for hours in order to make deadlines. I resigned myself to the possibility that at any moment I was going to collapse from exhaustion.

"And how are you doing, Turrútut?"

For a second, I didn't recognize that strange sound. It had been months since we had uttered it over the phone. I had also forgotten what it was like for Alex to reciprocate, to inquire about *my* emotional state.

"Me?" I said, uncertainly.

"Yes, who else? How are *you* doing?"

I must have been waiting for his permission, because I opened the floodgates and everything came pouring out: the still uncertain medical diagnosis, the shitty relationship, my weight gain, my isolation, the stress on my finances, and the exertion from taking on too many freelance projects that left me moving about with only a few hours of sleep and not enough energy to even masturbate. I had become this workaholic alcoholic who had buried himself like a mole in order to avoid facing the hard truth that before I could do something like take care of my little brother, I had to take care of myself.

Maybe Alex hadn't expected such a thorough response, but he got it anyway.

"Why didn't you tell me any of this?" he said. "I've been spilling my guts out on the phone every time, and you just kept holding out? I feel like an asshole."

"Don't, please don't, Alex. I wasn't ready. I had to get to that place. It's always like that with me. I have to hit rock bottom first."

"Well, okay, but that didn't sound like rock bottom; that sounded like fucking hell."

I couldn't resist a chuckle, which made him laugh as well. That was the first time in a long while that we had laughed with each other, and it felt refreshing, rejuvenating.

"I mean, I imagine you dragging your ass off to work looking like the hunchback of Notre Dame."

I followed his lead. "And I imagine you dragging your knuckles on the ground like a bloated gorilla."

"Isn't it time to ring the church bells?"

"No, it's show time at the circus. Don't forget to wear your fez."

We kept piling on the teasing until I had tears in my eyes. And when the laughter finally died down, my brother said, "Do you think our parents would've been disappointed with the mess we made of our lives?"

"We have to stop looking at ourselves like that, Turrútut. We got fucked over badly—no parents, no inheritance, no other relatives to ask for help—but we didn't end up drug dealers or in prison. I don't think we did all that bad considering."

"Well, you did alright. You're a professor and a writer. That's something."

"And you're a good father and a good man. That's something too."

"Maybe this is how we should have started our conversation all those months ago."

"Or maybe it took all those other conversations to get to this one. I think this is how it goes, Turrútut. For everyone."

After a brief moment of reflection, Alex said, "So now what?"

"Now comes the next day, except we're not alone. It's the two of us now; we have to look out for each other."

"You mean you shouldn't have to be my substitute father just because you're my older brother."

"No, I mean we have to look out for each other. That's all."

Maybe the phrase I was looking for was "man up," but that implied that our mistakes were a result of immaturity, and that wasn't true. We had been men all this time—flawed, imperfect, emotionally vulnerable. Our manhood was shaped by what our father taught us and what he didn't teach us, by his presence and his absence, by those things he did and what he couldn't do for his two oldest sons. But brotherhood—that was shaped by the two of us from the very beginning, and that relationship was still in progress.

I wasn't sure exactly how that was going to work out, but it felt like the best way to let my brother know I needed some time to work through my health issues. We also had to figure out a monthly allowance that wasn't going to leave me bankrupt, and we had to stop wallowing in our setbacks and start changing our attitudes—those around us would appreciate it. Shifting directions wasn't easy. It didn't happen in a week and it didn't happen in a month. But we eventually reached a place during our weekly check-ins that offered us some hope, if not some peace of mind.

"How are things going between you and Guadalupe?"

"It's going. We're talking more. We still fight, but we're not making stupid threats like before. How about you? How are things going with you?"

"I lost a little weight finally. I had to give up drinking, but I don't miss it, to tell you the truth. In fact, it feels great not to have to depend on alcohol."

"Yeah, I cut back on the drinking too. Trying to quit altogether," Alex said. "What would our father say about that?"

"That's just another one of those things we will never know," I said. "And maybe it's better that way. But back to us."

"Yes, back to us."

A Oaxaca Journal

Días de los Muertos. The Days of the Dead. I traveled here to the colonial city of Oaxaca to pay tribute to my parents as if honoring them on Mexican soil gave my gesture more meaning. I should have gone to Michoacán, our home state, but I wanted to situate myself at the center of Mictlán, the land of the dead. No other place in México builds a more convincing stage than Oaxaca: Each restaurant, hotel, and shop places a human-sized Catrina as skeleton hostess at the entrance to welcome clients and guests. Sugar skulls, altars fiery with orange marigolds, clusters of young people in painted skeleton faces strolling the cobblestones—everything and everyone is complicit in the theater. Even the bread. Pan de muerto. Bread of the dead.

At breakfast at the hotel restaurant, I sit beneath the flat screen TV to avoid looking at it, though I can hear the sounds of gunfire. The station is showing a typical American detective show dubbed in Spanish. I praise my choice when I notice that a pair of diners seated at the next table can't resist glancing over once in a while as they chat. Suddenly one of them says to the other, "Look, look! You see that? That's an American cemetery."

Though I know exactly what I am going to see, I still look up at the funeral scene taking place among a row of nondescript headstones, each indistinguishable from the next, dramatically different from the Mexican cemeteries with their colorful tiles and angel statues presiding over flowers at every stage of decay.

"How ugly," declares the second diner. "How do they even find the grave they're looking for?"

"Maybe that's the point," says the first, mischief in her voice. "Maybe they bury them there to lose them." And they burst out laughing.

I laugh too because that is the kind of dark Mexican humor I came looking for, the kind that makes the pain a little more tolerable. Isn't that the whole point to the Days of the Dead? To smile in the face of absence and loss? I lost my mother and my father young. She died when I was twelve. He died when I was thirty-six, though he abandoned me when I was thirteen. I have just turned forty-five. Their deaths are so far away, yet I still sob for them with the same adolescent fervor.

On the first night in Oaxaca, I fall asleep to the sounds of a brass band and fireworks. I am exhausted from the journey, but I still feel a sense of freedom to do nothing but rest and then focus on my mission. Outside, so much joyful screeching and cheering. And then I wonder: Is there room among the merriment for the size of my grief?

After breakfast, I walk down the main cobblestone road, Macedonio Alcalá. It unsettles me because that was my mother's maiden name. Now I see and hear the name—Restaurante Alcalá, Galería Alcalá, Calle Alcalá—repeatedly during my stay. Santo Domingo church towers majestically over the road, and the artisan shops line both sides of the street all the way down to el zócalo, the main city square. I have been collecting Day of the Dead imagery since I left México at the age of ten. Now I collect Day of the Dead art— expensive items that I never dreamed I could own. Back then, all I kept were the cheap trinkets that cost only a few pesos because only a few pesos was all I had to spend during my family's yearly trip back to México.

My eyes light up each time I walk into the small paradise of Mexican folk art. I remind myself that I can't possibly fit another item in my overcrowded studio apartment in Queens, but this is just a formality since it has never stopped me from purchasing yet one more thing. *It can sit on the windowsill or hang on the kitchen door*, I reason, justifying my decision. No matter how large, I envision a place for it.

Guests to my apartment always marvel at my collection of Mexican folk art. At first. At first, it was fun to say how it was like checking into a gallery, how it was like sleeping in a museum. But once they realize they have to walk with extreme caution to avoid knocking down a piece of pottery or bumping into a display stand, they begin to make suggestions about downsizing or rearranging the items in order to clear a path to the bathroom. Here I scoff at their criticisms and say something rude like "You know where there's plenty of space to move around? A hotel room."

I collect. I accumulate. Not necessarily hoarding, but I am headed there. Once, an ex-boyfriend said, "The thing about waking up here is that there's always a pair of eyes on me." As I choose three more masks for my wall, each one so unique in its artist rendering of pre-Columbian iconography, the truth of that statement haunts me. Eyes on papier-mâché skulls, on beaded masks, on faces made of clay and wood, on paintings. But no photographs of people. I don't have a single family photograph on display because I have so precious few that I keep them only for private viewing.

The truth is I've been robbed of the pleasure of keeping photographs most of my life. When my mother died, I was too young to wonder about what became of her personal cache of photographs. My father remarried and moved away, and after he died, I imagined that his cache rightly belonged to his daughters, like that photograph of my parents taken soon after their marriage: she, still a teenager, her head slightly tilted toward my father's shoulder; he in his early twenties, broke and likely wondering how much this studio portrait was going to cost him. I claimed it once, and then my father fought me for it, so I gave it back. Who knows what my half sisters did with it after coming across this image of their recently deceased father posing lovingly with a woman who died long before they were born?

My paternal grandparents, who raised me in California, are also gone, and I know for certain that their memorabilia was claimed by their only daughter, an aunt I no longer spoke to after she became a born-again Christian and disowned me because I was gay. My access has been nil to most of the photo images of my youth, of my family, of our history in Michoacán before our various migrations north to California.

I remember with plenty of envy those afternoons my grandparents would sit on the couch and sift through thick family albums and boxes of black-and-white or sepia pictures that for some inexplicable reason were not set into albums. There they were, a community of stand-alone images, the curve of the paper becoming more pronounced with age, like old people's backbones.

If she wasn't too lost in thought, Abuela would answer my questions about people and places from an era in México when such things as cameras and visits to the portrait studio were improbable luxuries, especially for poor families like the González clan. It was surprising that they had any of these keepsakes at all.

"That's Marina," I screeched once, impressed that I could identify a younger, thinner version of my cousin. Abuela affirmed my guess. That was also one of my favorite photographs. Abuela, her youngest son, Ramón, only a teenager then, and little Marina had been traveling through Mexico City. There was a photographer in the main square with a large drawing of an airplane on a stretch of plywood. Openings had been cut out in the shape of windows, and people could stand behind the wood and poke their heads through as if they were passengers on this make-believe flight.

It never dawned on me to ask whose idea it was to pose for this funny picture. Was it a whim from Tío Ramón, who usually got his way? Or did little Marina make this childish request? Or maybe it was Abuela herself, knowing that this photograph would make her giggle many years later. I was never to find out because Abuela died, and that photograph vanished in the string of ownership changes. But I still remember it. And the photograph now lives in the memory of Abuela on the couch with me sitting beside her, absorbing the heat of her amusement.

My entire apartment in Queens is not a gallery or a museum. It is an altar. And I place myself inside it as one more symbol connecting life to death. My body is what is left of my mother and my father on this earth. Yet I don't blame them for its hard-won journey: a lifelong struggle with eating disorders, a number of battles with drug and alcohol addiction, and its current vulnerability to a mysterious neurological disorder that's slowly wearing me down. I give my parents credit for my body's will to fight. Perhaps that is why I chose to come to Oaxaca during muertos season — to take myself out of the altar, to stand outside of it and see it with fresh eyes. What have I been living inside all these years?

Raising an altar is an art. All of them have to have the four elements represented, usually flowers (earth), incense (air), tequila or mezcal (water), and lighted candles (fire). The rest is personal expression. Here, in the artisan shops of Oaxaca, the altars are highly creative with the artist's unique flourish depending on his or her artistic medium or specialization. A potter molds clay into flowers and skulls, and then lines the tiers of the display with jugs and vases, the entire altar looking like a terra cotta showroom. A textile worker creates a wall-sized postcard by layering woven cloth bearing images of lilies, skeletons, and candles. Restaurants highlight perishable fruit and kitchen specialties. The altar at the church features religious imagery. Hotels built their altars around one of their paintings, usually of the Spaniard it was named after. This week, the next generation of Oaxacan artists pay tribute to revolutionaries: Villa, Zapata, and Che Guevara. Many small boutique altars honor previous owners or founders, their pictures prominently displayed at the top. I take picture after picture of these altars, sharing them on social media. And I think, how unfortunate that the digital age arrived long after my parents died. Whenever friends of mine share photographs of their visits home to see their aging parents, I become jealous. My mother died at age thirty-one, my father at age fifty-eight. Their faces remain frozen in my memory, and it's impossible to imagine them as elderly. If anything, it is I who am aging on their behalf, surpassing my mother's age at the time of her death and, with each passing day, nearing my father's age at the time of his. I am to become the old person each of them never had a chance to be.

On All Saints' Day, I decide to follow the crowds to the cemetery, though my dead are not buried there. My mother was buried in Michoacán, though this being many years later, two other bodies have been stacked on top of her grave. She herself was laid to rest on top of her grandmother. Cemetery real estate has become so precious that these high-rises are a necessity. I have been expecting those same tomb monstrosities in Oaxaca but am pleasantly surprised that the walls surrounding the large cemetery have been turned into mausoleum crypts that house the remains of the dead. Each crypt has been adorned with a candle: the winking flames cast a peaceful glow over the walkways and the shadowy visitors who pass by them in polite silence. I walk past all four walls, paying my respects to the thousands resting there. The center of the cemetery with its clutter of tombstones is at peace, undisturbed and invisible in the darkness.

My father was not buried. He was cremated, a choice I talked him into after Abuelo died and my aunt insisted he be buried. It was a costly expense to do so in California, but no one could talk her out of it. Abuela was particularly upset because the money came from Abuelo's bank account, which meant it would cut into the funds she had inherited. The rest of us knew that once Abuelo was buried, none of us would visit. He was such an ornery man that we hesitated reaching out to him while he was still alive. Dead, he was easily dismissed.

When Abuela died, she was buried right beside Abuelo and his bristly mustache. And that pained me because she died always wishing she could go back to Michoacán. I thought it might have been appropriate to send her remains back to her homeland, but that didn't happen. Not with my aunt in charge. So when my father died, I made sure that I had a voice in the matter. My aunt didn't intrude. His ashes were handed over to his second wife. I also gave her the money I didn't spend on a funeral or a burial. I thought that maybe my stepmother would do the appropriate thing and scatter his ashes in Michoacán, but she didn't. She scattered them in the backyard of their house in Mexicali on the U.S.-México border. None of these burials had that poetic end I envisioned for them. And that's the most honest reason I didn't go to Michoacán for the Days of the Dead.

After my stroll inside the cemetery, I walk out into a flurry of activity since the night has turned the street into a fair with amusement rides, carnival games, and a row of enterprising women who set up pop-up kitchens to prepare quesadillas, tacos, and tlayudas. At first, I scoff at the opportunism of the whole thing, but then I sit myself down and order a quesadilla stuffed with flor de calabaza—my favorite ingredient. I take a photograph of the woman heating the tortilla over the metal disc of a brasero. I devour it and order another.

The walk back is lonely for some reason. Without intending to, I have chosen an isolated route back to my hotel. Once in a while, I see a few young people, most of them in painted faces that make them look like pandas in the shadowy streets as they head toward the zócalo, where the brass bands are in full comparsa mode. This is a celebration for the young who dance into the late hours of the morning, tossing back shots of mezcal and documenting the night every fifteen minutes with selfies. I walk into my room, shower, climb into bed, and lie awake.

Middle-aged, I have become an early riser. When Abuela used to tell me she only slept four hours or so, I was in disbelief because she would go to bed around 7:00 p.m., sometimes even earlier. She was usually up by 4:00 a.m., stirring sugar into her coffee.

"So what do you do in bed all that time?" I asked.

"I think," she said.

Abuelo, on the other hand, slept all night. His loud snoring was evidence of that, and I felt bad that Abuela had to lie next to this noise for hours, doing her thinking. But I understand her now. The night owl in me became exhausted from that habit of staying up past midnight, a bad habit begun in my college days. Once I became a creature of the light, my body felt relieved. Now I am in bed by 10:00 p.m., sometimes sooner, and I usually fall asleep by 11:00 p.m., only to wake up at 5:00 a.m. Awake in bed, I do my thinking. I never asked Abuela what she thought about night after night, but I suspect it was not the kind of thinking that kept her awake, but rather the kind of thinking that helped her get some rest. I too sift through the rubble of what has happened this day or yesterday or the year before, in order to make peace with it.

The mornings in Oaxaca during the Days of the Dead are still and quiet, a stark contrast to the festive evenings. I dress in my exercise clothes and walk out for a brisk stroll. The young man behind the hotel counter is polite about unlocking the front gate though I can tell he had been partying most of the night by the way he fumbles half-awake with the keys. The streets are empty except for a few elderly folk who stick to their routines and sweep the sidewalks with large branches that function effectively as brooms. I reach El Llano, the small public park, and do my laps. Not a single soul joins me, not even the stray dogs.

As I circle around, I am secretly thrilled to have the entire park to myself, and then, just as quickly, I am startled at how I have turned into Abuelo. He was a cranky old man who liked to be around people less and less. I always said that he would have been happier had he remained single, wifeless, and childless, setting a schedule that took into consideration nobody's needs but his own.

And then another thought seizes me. I came to Oaxaca to honor my parents, yet I have been thinking about my grandparents much more. Perhaps because my own parents were not such a large part of my life, not since adolescence. My grandparents, on the other hand, got to see me stumble into adulthood. If I was identifying family resemblances and shared traits through them, it was because they were my points of reference—not my mother, not my father.

I sit on a nearby bench as this revelation weighs on me. What am I holding onto then with that altar in Queens? To the never was? To the could have been? A sure sign that what was, what had been, has left me wanting, dissatisfied.

The last time I visited my maternal grandparents in Michoacán, I came across a cosmetics case that my mother had brought with her on her final visit, shortly before she passed away. I was more interested in holding the things that had felt her touch but was pleasantly surprised to come across a small stack of pictures—of me as a child accompanying my family on the California grape boycott marches of the 1970s, of my parents dating as teenagers, of my father in his twenties, of our only visit to Disneyland as a family. I knew not to ask for them, so I borrowed half a dozen and had them reproduced at the nearby portrait studio.

"You are too young to keep things like these," my grand-mother argued when I asked for permission to copy them. I was in my twenties at the time.

"But I don't have any of my own," I pleaded. "I want something to remember her by."

She relented, and even though I had simply made copies, it seemed that I had cheapened their value, or at least sullied their uniqueness somehow. I stored away the photographs in a small box and rarely looked at them after that. I wasn't sure if this was because I wasn't used to having these kinds of keepsakes or because I knew they had been hidden from me all that time and so they would never really be mine. How troubling it was for my grand-mother that I should take something that she had inherited from her oldest daughter. How troubling it was for me to add them to the baggage of things that followed me whenever I moved.

There was one other photograph that came to me by accident. It was a picture of my mother, my brother, and me, posing in front of La Villa in Mexico City. It was taken on our first airplane ride, on my mother's final trip to the homeland. My mother, having survived her open-heart surgery, wanted to thank her guiding saint, La Virgen de Guadalupe. It was surprising to see how tiny my mother looked. I wasn't even a teenager, yet I was already taller and thicker. She stood, thinner than I remembered her, between my brother and me, that telltale grimace on her face, an expression made permanent by the stroke she had suffered earlier in the year. In a few months, she would be dead and buried in Michoacán.

But the remarkable feature on that photograph was the ciga-rette burn above her head, deliberately placed there by the smoker who held this picture in his or her hands. The mark was too cen-tered, too precise to have been accidental. It was a cruel, destruc-tive gesture. The photograph had been buried among a stash of clothing. When one of my aunts discovered it, she gave it to me discreetly, expressing concern about that malicious act and complete bewilderment about who might have done it.

"It's rightly yours," she said to me. "You're the oldest. You have to tell your children your mother's story."

"And what do I say about that burn?" I asked sheepishly. My aunt just shook her head.

I still have the photograph, but no children. Over the years, I have often thought about surrendering it to my brother, but I hesitate each time. His wife and children never knew our mother, who died when my brother was only eleven. This photograph, like all the other ones I keep stored in my apartment, was destined to meet the same fate that my father's belongings met after his death: disappearing into the hands or caprices of person or persons unknown. No saving grace awaits the González family heirlooms after death. I imagine those faces, dissociated from their identities and stories, anonymous and blank—two-dimensional relics in a bargain bin at a secondhand store, at best. At worst, discarded paper.

On the eve of All Souls' Day, Oaxaca is in full party mode, but the energy is no more intense than the previous night. Revelers recover enough to repeat their antics, and the streets fill up with crowds and brass bands whose tunes animate the extroverts to dance, the tuba punctuating the stomping. My somber mood keeps me from joining in. Down at the zócalo, the book fair tents showcasing authors and literature panels are coming down, and a crew of young people passes out flyers announcing the next cultural happening—a film festival at the historic Teatro Macedonio just a few blocks away. I take a schedule of the screenings and resolve to attend at least one of the showings, but at the moment, I have more pressing needs—to sate my hunger.

Only in México do I have the courage to enter a restaurant alone. I am not self-conscious about dining solo, and neither do I feel any judgments from the other diners. This isn't something I feel comfortable doing in NYC, though I have seen people eating alone there on many occasions. But as a New Yorker, dining out without company feels like an admission of loneliness. Somehow, as a tourist, this act doesn't seem so devastating.

I take a seat at one of the more upscale bistros on Alcalá, and the server immediately swoops in to give me attention. He is handsome, and his dark complexion reminds me of my father. This is a typical connection for me; I seem to always be looking for my father in the faces of middle-aged Mexican men. Although in situations like this, the resemblance is immediately broken by the exaggerated politeness and deference in the voices of the servers. My father was loud, imposing, and given to fits of laughter that showed his entire upper row of teeth.

I order the mole poblano and a salad with nopales and flor de calabaza. No mezcal for me. That will come later, at the curandero's house. A friend of mine had told me about this faith healer whose massages were designed to relieve physical and emotional stress simultaneously. He was having a get-together—a kind of spiritual healing—for his frequent clients at the nearby town of Guadalupe Hidalgo, and my friend had talked him into allowing me to attend though I had never been his client. I keep glancing at my watch, more and more nervous about the taxi ride to the outskirts of town to a place so isolated, part of the directions read: "You will go down a winding road with no street lights for about twenty minutes."

As I leave the restaurant, one of the famous Oaxacan calendas is winding its way down from Santo Domingo. I had seen these oversized lanterns and giant papier-mâché figures as part of wedding party processions, but tonight it is just one more current of energy streaming downtown. Nothing gets in the way of a calenda, and it brings traffic to a frustrating halt. By the time I manage to find a taxi driver who will agree to give me a few hours of his time, I am so relieved that my nerves about the impending trip dissipate.

The farther the taxi travels out of town, the darker the streets. By the time we reach the unpaved roads, my anxiety kicks in again, though I am careful not to show it. Suddenly, just when I begin to suspect I might have led the driver to the middle of nowhere, a town springs into view.

Perhaps I expected to find myself in some quaint rural village with burro carts and women with thick braids clad in rebozos, the curandero's residence a wooden shack slightly removed from the community because it has been given its place of prominence, like a church. Instead, the town is rather modern, with paved roads, cement buildings, and an internet café. The curandero's house looks no different from the others with its iron gate that opens to an enclosed courtyard where the taxi driver parks next to a truck that looks like it has just come out of the factory. And the curandero, Alejandro, a handsome man with blue-green eyes, greets me with a firm handshake. He looks no older than me.

Alejandro's sister gives the taxi driver a cup of chocolate to drink as he waits patiently to drive me back to the city. There are a few other guests, but the conversation revolves around mutual acquaintances, and the only effort to include me is occasional eye contact as they gossip. Outside, the town's comparsa marches by and everyone rushes to the gate to catch a glimpse of the costumes the young people have been working on all year to show off at this parade. Indeed, the costumes are impressive and well thought-out. Small parties of threes and fours have coordinated their outfits, many made with colored spongy material shaped into monsters that resemble those from video games and not the famous *alebrijes* so popular with folk art collectors.

"They will go at it until dawn," Alejandro says.

"Well, it's only for one night," I say, by way of condoning the partying.

"Just one night?" he replies. "This is day two. This goes on for a week in the towns."

I grow weary simply knowing that the young people will walk from one corner of the street to the next, hour after hour, dancing and cheering until the bright morning sun sends them home.

The spiritual healing itself feels more like a counseling session, with people checking in and reporting their progress—that depression, this marital discord. Pan de muerto is passed around, as well as instant coffee and mezcal, poured as each person shares a moment of unburdening. We sit in Alejandro's living room. His altar, very unassuming with simple candles and a few pieces of fruit over the different tiers, sits snugly between the sofa and the television.

When my turn comes to speak, I don't have much to say except to introduce myself, a stranger who has come from so far away to infiltrate the communal therapy of people who clearly have meaningful relationships with one another. I feel awkward, as if I had walked into a support group and had been too embarrassed to leave. What would my host think if he knew that I had expected a smoky room that smelled of burning copal, a pre-Columbian ritual with sacred water sprinkled with sage and performed by an ancient curandero dressed in indigenous garb? What film had planted that romanticized version of Mexican folk healing in my head?

I babble on incoherently until I notice the disinterest in other people's eyes, and so I simply stop. No one protests, not even Alejandro, who looks anxious to move on. He offers a prayer that sounds more Catholic than Amerindian and then invites everyone to place the photographs of departed loved ones on the altar. Framed photographs pop out of handbags and backpacks. I feel even more like an interloper because that detail had not been relayed to me, so I sit there motionless as everyone steps forward, a few breaking into tears as they kiss the faces of those who have left them behind. Suddenly the altar, now populated by more faces foreign to me, seems farther away.

"And where are your dead?" the curandero asks me. And the question is too complicated to answer in a simple sentence. So I express myself the only way I know how. I cry, an unashamed release, and I feel a great sorrow spill out: the grief over my many losses—my parents, my grandparents—the regret of those unwise decisions in my youth that I suspect have come back to take their toll on my ailing body, the loneliness that comes with being an orphan, the isolation that comes with depression, and the burden of having to carry everyone else's stories because I'm the one who survived. And all this time I had been doing the Days of the Dead all wrong. Instead of opening up, I had been shutting in. Instead of standing in front of my altar, I had stepped inside it. Celebrating the Days of the Dead is an act of permission to keep living, to nod at death as a form of respect for the hard truth that all things come to an end. That truth also recognizes the suffering and torment of loss, but it is not meant to seize the soul year-round, rather only for a day or two. The point is to remember. Remember death. Remember life.

As I climb into the taxi and instruct the driver to head back to Oaxaca, I am amused that my lesson was learned not in the whimsical Mictlán as I had expected but in this unassuming little town I had never heard of and am likely never to see again. Yet I am filled with gratitude and a renewed sense of purpose as I imagine redecorating my apartment in Queens to make it look less like a tomb and more like a living space.

Just then, as the driver turns onto the main road, another taxi catches up with us and its driver lowers his window. "Check your back tire! Something's wrong!"

My driver looks at me through the rearview mirror and quips: "I better pull into the next gas station. I wouldn't want to get us killed. There's a ravine here that swallows entire buses, and no one's ever heard from again."

I lean my head out the window to the side of the road, and there it is: the plunge into the netherworld. On any other night I might have pressed my body against the seat, paralyzed with panic. But not on this one. This is the night I let go of the fear of letting go.

FAMILY OUTING

When I told my brother that I wanted to go to the beach during my visit, I imagined he understood I longed for a touristy spot where I could set up my towel and suntan lotion within walking distance of a *palapa* bar. I wanted to show off the improvement on my body—thirty pounds lighter and with upper torso musculature I never imagined I would ever achieve, certainly not in my midforties. I was also celebrating my sixth month without a cane. After seven years with a crutch, it was an exhilarating triumph. Instead, Alex took me to a more private area that looked more like a desert than a beach. I walked over the dried skeleton of a bird to get the edge of the water lined with smooth stone pebbles and the occasional seashell. Guadalupe and Halima, who had just turned sixteen, stayed back in the shade of the only straw hut left standing; all the others had tipped over from neglect. André, only a few months shy of seven, already knew how to unfurl the heavy net my brother would spend the next four hours casting from the shore while I baked in the sun. I made the best of it, appreciating the quiet, drifting into daydream as I watched Alex's tenacity with his arduous task that netted only a few fish by the end of the day. But it was the exercise that kept him going, he said, and the reminder that there was something so grand and beautiful. I was surprised by the romanticism of his comment. But it made me appreciate his new life in this fishing village on the Sea of Cortez, considered the richest body of water on the planet. And when a cobalt blue fish came close to the edge, I lost my words and simply pointed at it as if that were enough to pin it down long enough for my brother to run over with the net.

"Here! Here!" I blurted out finally.

Alex slowly gathered the net weighed down by sinkers and dragged it through the water. By the time he was close, that dazzling fish had darted back into the depths of the sea.

"A bit late, Turrútut," I said.

Alex laughed. "That was a dorado. You should have tried to grab it. Or knocked it unconscious with a shoe."

"At least I got to see one," I said, shaking off my brother's silliness. "I've never seen such a gorgeous color."

"Now you can write a poem about it. See? The trip will be worth more than sunburn."

I checked my shoulders and chest. They had reddened, but they didn't hurt like the area just below my receding hairline. I wasn't looking forward to the next day.

During lunch hour, I insisted on eating with my brother on the beach. He refused to leave the fishing poles he had cast just in case something bit. André joined his mother and sister beneath the hut.

"This is paradise," I said. Saguaros sprawled across the foot of the mountain behind us. The stark contrast to my brother's previous residence at the impoverished El Rancho prompted me to ask if he had heard from our stepmother, Amelia, or her children.

"Not really," he said. "Although I did hear something interesting about Mari, Tío Rafael's widow. Remember her?"

It had been awhile but yes, I did remember the plump lady who put up with our temperamental uncle's shenanigans until his death. "What about her?"

"Turns out she moved in with Amelia for a bit, until she sold the house and moved back to wherever she was from."

"The two González widows living together? Well, that's quite a plot twist."

I couldn't wrap my head around it, but I supposed the two women had to do what they could to survive. All the Gonzálezes who had once lived there were gone, dead or relocated. They were the last people to arrive, and yet there they were, the last two still standing. And now it was only Amelia, her five children spread out in different residences on the same block, repeating a pattern they must have learned from the González clan—stay close enough to each other in order to keep an eye on things and then talk shit about them.

"That's pretty rich territory to write about right there," I concluded.

After a pause, Alex changed the subject. "Let me ask you, Turrútut, did you always want to be a writer?"

I tried to explain that the easy answer was yes, because that's what I grew to love. But the truth was that when I first fantasized about being a writer, I thought writers remained hidden away, that only their labor came to light by way of publication. If I had known then that a writer had to stand in front of people as often as I had, I would have chosen a different profession. I was much too shy for this one.

"Like what?" my brother pressed. "What else did you want to do?"

I wasn't sure what my brother was searching for, but it was making me nervous. Did I have an honest answer for that? As we munched on ceviche tostadas, I considered the question. A teacher was what I always told myself, and others. I wanted a life near books, the only places that gave me comfort. Though at one time I fantasized about being an actor—a capricious dream I became embarrassed to admit later, though in fact this was another effort at escape from the person I didn't want to be. The gay boy could hide in the silence of being a reader, or a nerd, or a character. A profession was more than a purpose; it was a disguise.

"I guess I'm doing what I always wanted now," I said. "To be out in the open. Without fear."

Suddenly Alex shot up from his chair and grabbed the fishing pole. He had kept his eye on the line the entire time. But after he reeled it in, there was nothing caught in the hook. He grabbed the bait and jiggled what looked like a toy at me.

"I made this myself," he said, proudly.

I had the impulse to poke fun at him, to say, "Well, I guess it sucks, doesn't it?" But I held back.

"Don't worry, it works sometimes," he said, as if reading my mind. I laughed.

After he threw the line again, I turned the question over to him.

"Me? I don't know. A football player. A drug lord. El Chapo."

I rolled my eyes. "No, seriously."

"A wrestler."

"A wrestler? Like, an Olympic wrestler?"

"Nah, like a World Wrestling Federation wrestler. Like André the Giant. He was my hero. Why do you think I named my son after him? Just don't go telling Guadalupe."

I didn't want to know if he was kidding or not, so I let it slide, especially because it was me who had come up with such a poetic name for his daughter.

Once he stopped giggling, he looked out into the water. "I guess I'm doing what I always wanted too. To be out in the open. Without fear."

We were using the same words but we were talking about very different experiences: my sexuality, his freedom, the prisons we both endured locked up in our family's houses and inside that ugly designation, orphan. After our mother died, relatives lined up to offer to take me in. I was the quiet one, the obedient one. But Alex was the rambunctious one. When my aunts offered to take me in without him, I refused. I didn't want to be separated from my brother, even if we didn't get along much. The only person who agreed to take us both in was Abuelo, but we knew he had ulterior motives—the social security check that came with taking in the two orphans, as long as we stayed in school. I managed it, but my brother dropped out, and so he was tossed out of that house as well. What a terrible thing to feel unwanted. I understood that more than anyone, and so I kept my sexuality a secret. But now, both of us men in our forties, we didn't have to cower any longer. We were free.

"Maybe we're free because everybody's dead," I said out loud.

My brother turned to me, aware that this was another one of my episodes in which I got lost in thought and then uttered statements without context. He wiped his hands on his shorts and turned to his net, resuming his casting and dragging. By early afternoon, the tide began to stretch more noisily up the shore.

All this time, not a single soul came to this part of Alex's beach. Perhaps because it was a weekday or because it was so isolated and there was nothing attractive about a spot nowhere near any amenities. If anyone had to pee, well there was the water—one just had to make sure to go in waist deep. This really was my brother's paradise, where the only inhabitants at the moment were his immediate family and his brother from the big city who kept taking shirtless selfies and sending them to his ex-boyfriends, expecting compliments.

"Okay, supermodel," Guadalupe chided. "Help me carry the cooler to the truck."

I felt the sting of the heat at various points on my skin. "How long does he plan to stay out here?"

"All night, if he had his way. You're lucky we all came. Once he starts hearing the kids whining, he loses his patience. He knows that time is coming soon, so let me start packing up."

We lifted the cooler onto the truck bed and then pushed it forward. As Halima and André folded the chairs outside of earshot, I took advantage of the opportunity to speak privately with my sister-in-law.

I touched her arm. "Hey, I'm glad you and Alex are still together."

"Well, of course we are; why wouldn't we be?" she said defensively, and I knew then that Alex had never told her that I knew everything that had transpired between them. I also promised him I would keep that to myself, but it took so much effort to drown out the memory of those hurtful exchanges between them.

"Well, I'm just glad you're looking well," she said. "Alex told me you were falling apart. You look like you have a few more years left."

"Oh, I suspect I may have more than that," I said. "I have to keep my eye on things."

Not until that moment did I realize that I still held her partly responsible for my brother's breakdown, for not doing enough when she was right next to him the entire time. It was unfair of me to place such blame, but I couldn't help it. Men like my abusive Abuelo and my pitiful father had wives who stuck with them; why shouldn't my brother, who was like neither of these men, deserve as much if not more?

Suddenly I remembered the call I had made to them from Venice. I was on a month-long artist residency to Italy and had been convinced to do something extra special during my birthday, my forty-third. My companion to the floating city was a young writer from the Philippines. We marveled at the traffic on the canals and walked the winding roads until nightfall, when the streets began to empty. It was he who had also convinced me to call my brother because this was a momentous occasion and I needed to reach back to my homeland, México. Enchanted by the trip and sentimental after a few glasses of champagne, I couldn't help myself. It would be a nice surprise for my family to hear from me all the way from Venice, I thought, and so I dialed. Guadalupe answered.

"I'm in Venice!" I yelled into the phone.

"Well, good for you," she said, in a tone that made me realize I had interrupted something important. "I wish I could let you speak to your brother, but I kicked him out."

My heart sank. "What? I don't understand."

"I kicked him out. So I need another man. Bring me back an Italian."

And then we got cut off. But I didn't feel like dialing again. My companion saw the look of devastation on my face, so he turned away to stare at the canal. A boat passed by with a group of revelers singing in a language I didn't know. They were drunk. One of them dropped a plastic cup overboard, and I wanted to scold him.

I shook the memory out of my mind and returned to Guadalupe, who looked quite annoyed.

"You don't have to keep an eye on things," she said. "That's my job."

"Oh, is it?" I snapped. "Well, one of those things is your man. Just so you know."

Her disdain made me ashamed I was letting my overprotectiveness become an exchange of cheap shots and innuendoes. I wanted to apologize, but she shifted her energy over to her children. In the distance, Alex kept casting his net, his last desperate attempts at snagging something. Guadalupe walked over to convince him to give up; Halima and André followed closely behind.

Now the family portrait was complete without me in it. This was my brother's most hard-won journey, this twenty-year marriage and fatherhood. My one sadness was that neither of our parents was alive to witness it. But I was. I was witnessing it. And as their bodies moved forward in unison, it was the most beautiful sight I saw that day.

The Wondrous Flight
of the Hummingbird

Do you remember Tzintzuntzán?"
"I don't," my brother says. "I don't remember Tzintzuntzán at all."

The name of the town at the northeast shore of Lake Pátzcuaro is pure onomatopoeia. Say it—Tzin-tzun-tzán—and a hummingbird zips by with each syllable. These elusive little birds are so fast they're invisible and can never be caged. In fact, the only way the people of Tzintzuntzán can attempt to capture a hummingbird is to carve one out of wood, or to sculpt one in iron. The only way for visitors to own one is to buy it. I brought two of them with me that hang from the kitchen doorway of my NYC apartment. As soon as I put them up, I realized how ridiculous this illusion was since the wings are frozen midflight and the bodies dangle from fishing lines because what I "caught" was nothing less than decorated dead weight. These are memorials to the fleeting hummingbird, a wondrous feathered creature whose population has been dwindling over the years. I saw hundreds of memorials in Tzintzuntzán, but not a single living example of what all that artistry honors. Still, it is difficult to challenge the town's name—it *is* the place of the hummingbirds. They are everywhere: on furniture, on pottery, and stitched near the hems of pretty little dresses. And each time I say the town's name, the hummingbird becomes audible—a ghost sound emanating from the vibrant depictions.

We will have to go, Turrútut, the next time we visit Michoacán, though I have no idea when it will be safe to do so again. The stories of the region's kidnappings are alarming, and what used to be a fear that belonged to other people in other parts of town is now ours as well—we have walked into our homeland's darkest alley and are still dealing with the anxiety of that encounter. What a tragedy to be denied entry to our childhood landscape, to imagine it wilt and wither without us as we pretend, quite stupidly, that it remains the same, unchanged because we are not in it. We must remain outside the place of first memory as if in exile. "It's safe to come here," our relatives tell us, but it never sounds convincing coming from people who never had to say the words we said that time when language died like flowers in our mouths, empty of hope and bloated with despair. How long before the nightmares ended? How long before you could climb into your car without reaching down beneath the seat to feel the comfort of the tire iron? How many years of life did you lose as you wandered through the streets in Mexicali in a crazed panic? How many years of life drained down to my feet as I stood there, waiting for news of your fate?

At the moment, my mobility continues to improve with this new therapy that includes painful shots of hormones and steroids. But the discomfort is worth it. I've even begun to jog again, something I had not been able to do in almost a decade. My muscle growth has astounded the doctors, who had simply wanted to slow down the loss of body mass, and there I was bulking up like a champ. I can feel the fit body that I buried many years ago inside this crippled one begin to surface, to reclaim its proper place in front of the mirror. I'm rebuilding my strength and my confidence, daring to flirt again, to venture into the passionate embraces of other men. Intimacy is so much more beautiful when it's not relegated to fantasy but a realized sensory experience with another being—when it is an expression without obstacle. I have found the pleasures I had forgotten and never thought I would ever have again. I'm in the throes of joy. I'm alive.

Those nightmares I sometimes still suffer from might seem ridiculous compared to what yours might be. In my darkest dreamscape, my cane snaps in two or sinks to the ground or is maddeningly out of reach, and it's this state of helplessness that makes me wake up and cry into my hands. Who will take care of me if the affliction returns? Now I understand, as you understand, that the hardest thing to admit is that you must take care of you. I must take care of me.

So what are we waiting for? Let's march directly to Michoacán as stubbornly as we have moved through our adult years. It's not blind luck that gets us through; it's the hard-won strength of our roughed-up spirits, the history of our battle scars. We haven't faced anything yet that can defeat us.

I remember that time you and our father drove all the way from El Rancho to Tempe, Arizona, to help me move. I was relocating from one cockroach-infested apartment on the east side to another one on the west, just as cockroach-infested. Except that I was now going to live alone, without roommates. It was a huge financial sacrifice for me, but it was necessary—I wanted the space to read and write without having to work around the schedules of the people I shared an apartment with. I wanted complete and uninterrupted access to my creativity. It was my final year of graduate school, and I had a thesis to finish—a novel about the California grape pickers, a book about our family's life of labor. I can't imagine if any of that factored into your decision to make that trek to Arizona, but I suspect that for our father it was paternal duty. You had both driven me to Riverside for my first college degree, and to

Davis for my second. I drove myself to Tempe, but now I needed help, and there you both were again.

I had a bed, boxes of books, and a small bureau I purchased from one of my neighbors. It was Apá's idea to bring a bookshelf. Or rather, to build one. He brought along the wood and a drill. Since it was the middle of the sweltering Arizona summer, we moved long after sundown, when the weather was still humid but tolerable. As we crossed the main drag in that scrappy truck, our father was stunned by all the foot traffic. "What the fuck are all these people doing out at this hour?" he said. "Don't they have homes?" I laughed at how foreign the concept of the college town appeared to him.

While Apá built the bookshelf, you and I unloaded, unpacked, and then we walked to the small store down the street to buy generic brands of canned vegetables and tuna, mayonnaise and bread. I didn't have a table, so we ate on our knees on the carpet. I was embarrassed that I didn't have any money to treat you to a nice meal at a restaurant, but neither of you minded.

"It's like those times we used to pick grapes together," Apá said. And we were transported back to the shade underneath the grape vines, where we would huddle around a small crate and eat the only meal of the day—beef and bean burritos that Abuela had packed at dawn. There was no place to wash our hands, so we ate dirt and sulfur, and if we had cut our hands with the shears, we tasted our blood.

"You sure have come a long way," Apá said as he looked around at my modest living quarters, and I beamed because that was as close as he got to an expression of pride. The following summer I would be just as broke, subsisting on rice and potatoes but reading a book a day in order to educate myself because I was determined to be the well-read writer that my professors wanted me to be. And what got me through that hardship was knowing that you and Apá had given me your blessing to pursue this unusual dream to become a writer. I felt it each time I saw that bookshelf. The tensions between our father and me kept me from thanking him for that and for all the other times he was a good father. I'm fortunate, however, that I still have you and that I can thank you for being a good brother. Everyone else is gone. It's only the two of us now. Let's not keep anything unsaid before it's too late, before there's only one.

"Do you remember your mother?" our father used to ask us, on those moments of sentimentality that said he had been thinking about her, missing her, and he wanted us to bring her memory back together—a collective energy that blossomed with language in the mouth instead of drowning its flowers with grief or sadness or loss.

Turrútut, do you remember our father? Do you remember that time you came to Tempe together? How you had opened a map in order to chart your itinerary back to Mexicali and wanted to find a route around Phoenix because it had been the most stressful and frightening part of your trip? But there was no way around the bustling city, so you drove right back through it. In the age before cell phones, I had to wait for hours before I found out you had made it safely to the border. So in the meantime, I sat down next to the telephone and wrote because that was the only form of prayer I knew.

The last time I visited you in Baja California Sur, I woke up at the crack of dawn each day to write, to do the work I was being paid to do, what in turn paid for that trip to visit México and many other places. As my visit came to an end, you asked if I needed to print my boarding pass. I said no, that I would do that at the airport.

"There are printers at the airport?" you asked, quite earnestly.

"Yes, of course," I replied, puzzled.

You scratched your chin. "When I drove a tour bus, those people were always so worried about printing their boarding passes; why did they make me drive around in circles until I found a printer for them?"

"When was the last time you were in an airport, Turrútut?"

You didn't hesitate with your answer: 1982.

That was the year our mother died. That was the year we all flew for the first time to México—a financial sacrifice meant to relieve the stress for our mother's body on her final trip back home. For our mother, it was her first and only flight. I always knew that, and I remembered how protective she was on the entire trip, how excited you were, how scared I was. But I didn't know until that moment that it had been your first and only flight as well.

I leaned back in my chair with a sense of shame because my passport was a cluster of stamps that told the story of my international travels—Singapore, Spain, Italy, Scotland, England, Switzerland, Lithuania, Brazil, Costa Rica, Panamá, México, México, México, México, México. When I looked at a world map, it wasn't as abstract to me anymore. And then I wondered if I had failed you yet again, from that day Abuela had suggested I take you with me to college, that in effect I should have finished raising you because it was my duty as your older brother.

And then your six-year-old son walked out of his bedroom, his eyes mischievous, so eager to engage with the surprises of the day. He walked right into your arms, and you received him, kissing the top of his head. "Ay, Tilico," you said, nicknaming him the way Abuela used to do to each of us, the way we nicknamed each other. The affection for your son—you had learned it from our parents, certainly, and it gave me permission to keep moving on my journey because you had your own and that was perfectly fine. And every once in a while, for a few precious moments—I had to make peace with this truth—we crossed paths like two hummingbirds descending on the same rosebush before zooming out of sight to their respective vanishing points in the sky.

MANPOWER

Abuelo was the picker. Apá was the packer. Alex and I took turns harvesting grapes and carrying the heavy boxes of fruit down the row to our father. We had started out a group of seven, but the foreman said the group was too large. So Tío Rafael, who was an exceptional packer, was asked to form his own group with Tío Ramón and Juvenal, our cousin. That made sense since that was also how we split up between two cars to get to the fields. We came together as a family again during lunch hour, but the rest of the day, Alex and I had to stand opposite of Abuelo, who reprimanded us at every turn. We worked too slowly. We talked too much. We left the grapes too shiny. Since his hearing wasn't very good, we learned to whisper and to catch the words through the dusty leaves, over the sound of the squeaky hinges on three pairs of scissors.

"What are you going to do with your first check?" Alex asked. This was a question our father had asked us almost every day that first week on the job. It was his way of encouraging us since we were going to give up most of our summer to farm labor. Abuelo had already made it clear we were not going to be allowed to vege-tate in front of the television when school was out. "*Al fil,*" he said. To the fields. Like every other kid who, at fourteen, was old enough to work.

When the task became tedious, when the heat became oppressive, we threw that question out as a way to keep going. No one was going to stop us from dreaming.

"I want to buy a pair of dress shoes that aren't made of plastic," I said.

"Plastic?" Alex said, pausing for a second.

"You know, fake. They make your feet sweaty and stinky. I hear them say that the ones made of leather keep your feet fresh."

"Okay, but what do you want leather shoes for? You're not going to the prom. You don't go out on dates. You have no girlfriend. You don't dance."

"Neither do you," I countered.

"So what do you want them for?"

I wanted to say that I wanted to feel like a man for once, but I didn't really know what I meant by that. I had seen pictures of Abuelo in his youth, his mustache so black and preened to perfection, showing off the tattoos on his forearm. He was wearing dress pants and a pair of shoes that shone so clean and new they made him look respectable, despite the tattoos. During Apá's days as a musician, he was also pictured with bright, shiny, patent leather shoes. All the glamour of their pasts was on display in the footwear. Their present was dirty sneakers and work boots. That was my present as well. I wanted to claim my moment of glamour.

"Take that box out," Abuelo barked. He was only visible from the waist down, but I could see how he pointed to a full box with the ends of his scissors. I imagined his mustache punctuating his severe expression underneath that hat he always wore when he stepped out of the house.

It was Alex's turn, so he crossed underneath the vines. The rustling reminded me of rain. An odd image to invoke in the near one-hundred-degree heat, the sand around my sneakers growing warmer by the hour. Another desert deception, like a mirage.

As soon as Alex was out of earshot, Abuelo began his griping. "I'm not sure what your brother is thinking, skipping school and running off with your good-for-nothing cousins. Without school, he's going to end up here, with us. He thinks this life is easy, well, he's about to find out."

I knew by now that Abuelo did not want a response, just a listener. I let his words dust each bunch in my hand as I inspected it and determined that it was ripe enough to pick and place in the box. One thing I did admire about Abuelo was how he dropped a bunch so fearlessly from as high as the vine, confident that it wouldn't fall apart, grapes bouncing off in all directions. When I asked Apá about this, he said that it was decades of skill. "And he doesn't give a shit anymore," he added. "He knows the packer has to clean it before it's packed."

Abuelo kept on: "And your father, running around with that woman, as if he were a teenager. Even you boys don't bring us that kind of trouble."

Trouble meant that Amelia, Apá's soon-to-be wife, was pregnant. I didn't particularly like her, but I liked Abuelo less, and I didn't appreciate any poison coming from his mouth, no matter where it was going. He voiced these things to me, to Abuela, but to no one else. He was cowardly that way.

"I need to use the toilets," I said, and walked away.

At the end of the row, Apá stood at the packing table, shifting his weight and shaking his leg. I knew how painful it was for him to stand all those hours from 6:00 a.m. to quitting time, sometimes as late as 2:00 p.m. He saw me coming and smiled. His dark skin looked even darker with that red shirt he was wearing.

"Where's Alex?" I asked.

"I told him to bring me some water. And I'm thinking, why don't you go get me some water too?"

I pursed my lips. I knew the code. It was our father's way of letting us stretch our legs, and to give us a break from Abuelo.

As I walked out into the dirt avenue toward the water truck, my body ached just watching people bend, then stand still as they picked grapes on the hot soil, the long sleeves of their flannel shirts covered in sulfur. My eyes became moist. I felt sorry for Abuelo and Apá and everyone else who had to do this an entire lifetime. I was not yet out of high school, but I was already certain this would not be my fate. All that talk about colleges in my homeroom got me excited, though I had not yet revealed to my family what my plans were for the near future. I didn't want anyone—especially Abuelo—to get in the way. But I wasn't too sure about Alex's fate now that he had dropped out of school.

"Save me some," I said to him as I approached.

"It tastes funny," he said.

"Everything tastes funny here. Even saliva." I poured water into the paper cone. In a few hours, when the cones were exhausted, there would be a single dirty cup sitting on top of the tank. At that point, nobody cared about hygiene and everyone passed the cup from mouth to mouth.

"And what are you going to do with your first check?" I said.

"I don't know. Save for a car."

"A car? With the little money we're going to make? You're going to start with a tire?"

"Or maybe a fucking bicycle, okay?"

I didn't take his snapping at me too personally. The heat gave all of us short tempers.

We each filled a cone of water to take to our father. We already knew where his paycheck was going—to the new baby.

"What kind of car?" I said, as a way of assuaging Alex's hurt feelings.

"A convertible. I want to ride with the top off."

Alex, with his baby mustache that would never grow beyond chicken scratches, was only fifteen, but he already knew how to drive. I wasn't sure how this came to be since I was a year older and had never even practiced getting behind the wheel of car. Driver's ed was still a semester away.

"Where would you go?" I asked.

"I don't know. I'd just go."

And I realized that this was his way of dreaming about leaving. I had been plotting my escape as well.

My father took the cones and threw the water into his mouth. He crushed them and dropped them at his feet. They looked so out of place there, white crinkled paper over a small graveyard of discarded fruit not good enough to pack. He smiled. My father had a handsome smile, but I resented it because he never got me braces, and my crooked upper row embarrassed me. When I was younger, I kept pleading until he finally shut me up by telling me that they would straighten themselves out naturally. "My teeth used to be uglier than yours, right, Apá?" And Abuelo agreed from the couch, complicit in the deceit.

When we took our places at the grapevine again, Abuelo was gone. Our respite from his supervision was extended.

"He hates to work, doesn't he?" I said.

"Yeah, and so he takes it out on all of us."

Usually it was Abuela who worked in the fields and Abuelo stayed home to cook. But his younger brother, Tío Justo, had come to visit from who knows where, and he wouldn't stop teasing his older brother about how he had become the woman in the marriage.

"You should lend him your aprons, María," he called out, and no one dared laugh. Tío Justo cackled at his own jokes for all of us.

Even my grandmother wasn't amused. She stood behind the stove, making faces, bothered that Abuelo had asked her to do the cooking, which she didn't like to do. Nor was she much good at it. We couldn't stand Abuelo, but we sure did appreciate his skills in the kitchen because Abuela's dishes were usually inedible.

Tío Justo was the only person who could shame Abuelo. He ridiculed Abuelo's belly, his bald spot, his lack of gold jewelry and flaccid muscles, and the fact that he didn't pay attention to young women anymore. At the supermarket, Tío Justo would goad him, elbowing him whenever a pretty young girl walked past them. Abuelo looked so awkward trying to keep up with his brother's ogling. The entire theater of masculinity was mortifying to all of us because my father never acted like that and neither did he expect us to.

And so here Abuelo was, trying to prove to his brother that he was still a man by coming to work and forcing Abuela to stay home, and I knew that neither of them was happy about the arrangement. It almost made me feel sorry for him, until I saw him walk back to his spot.

"Remember when someone we know bought exercise equipment to impress someone else we know?" I said to Alex. The mischief in my tone made me blush. We had reached that part of the day when we started making fun of Abuelo.

Alex giggled. "I certainly do. I still use it. All he did was remove the packaging."

"If you're ever that mean to me when we're old, Alex, I promise you I'm going to kick my nice leather shoe up your ass."

"And if you're as ridiculous as they are when you get old, I'm going to run your ass over with my convertible."

We couldn't contain our giggling. And it wasn't until Abuelo told us to cut it out that we slipped back into the coma of the hot weather.

At quitting time, we weren't as relieved as everyone because our car was parked the farthest. This was one of Abuelo's bright ideas: to show up before everyone else so that we could nab the best parking spot on the side of the road. Sometimes it paid off because the work route took us toward the road and we were the first to reach our car, but if the route took us away from the road, we had the longest trek to Apá's precious blue Mustang.

Sure enough, we were the last to leave. And just as we settled into the hot vinyl seats, another heartbreak: the car wouldn't start.

"Now what?" Abuelo said. He wiped a ring of sweat underneath his hat.

"I don't know," Apá said. "We have gas. Let me check under the hood."

As my father went out to inspect the problem, Abuelo went at it: "What does your father know about cars? He's always buying these useless pieces of junk. He never has any money to invest on something that's not going to leave us all stranded in the middle of the desert. And now with another mouth to feed on the way, he's going to be broke for the rest of his life."

Wound up by his own anger, Abuelo got out of the car to join my father.

"And what the fuck does *he* know about cars?" Alex said.

We were getting too sweaty in the backseat, so we got out as well, only to find Apá and Abuelo arguing as one pulled on this wire and the other yanked on that cable.

"This is a piece of shit car," Abuelo said.

"You're not being very helpful, Apá. Why don't you go back inside?"

Abuelo grumbled, but he did just that, though not before calling the obvious: "And keep your eye out for anyone passing by; maybe all we need is a jump."

"Do you want us to walk to the main road, Apá?" I said. And that's when the tears started welling up in his eyes. So he smiled as he wiped them away.

"Dude," Alex said.

"I didn't do anything," I said.

But I *had* done something. I had reminded him of what was upon us: Alex wasn't doing well in school, Apá was expecting another child with a woman I didn't want to accept as my future stepmother, Abuelo was inflicting his insecurities on all of us, and I was about to leave forever, though no one but me knew that. Or maybe my father did know—a parental intuition that told him he was about to lose his son. But at the moment, here we all were, stuck because my father bought the cheapest car he could afford. We had worked close to nine hours, and now he had to watch his sons beg for help from a stranger on the side of the road.

"This is not the kind of life I wanted for you," he said, weeping with his hands flat on the car.

The raised hood kept us hidden from Abuelo's sight, but neither Alex nor I knew how to comfort our father. We were not used to gestures of affection. That was not manly behavior. Alex kept knocking on my elbow with his fist, as if encouraging me to make the first move. But I didn't know what that move should be.

"Stop crying, Apá," I said. "Don't let your father see you." I couldn't help but blurt out a phrase my own mother had said to me many times when I became too emotional when my father was nearby. It felt useful but not right. "Alex and I will get help," I continued. "You wait here in case anyone passes by."

Apá's sniffling was the last sound we heard as we made our way to the main road. It was going to be a wait because these were the grape fields and it was past harvesting time. Even the stragglers had made it home by now. Our best hope was one of our kin, an undocumented alien taking the back roads for safety, or a driver who had made a wrong turn somewhere. The nearest pay phone was miles away at the closest gas station.

"What do you think is going to happen?" Alex said.

"Oh, don't worry, a truck will come by and give us all a lift to the gas station."

"No, I meant, about Apá."

"Oh," I said. I looked behind us. Abuelo was looking our direction as if that could make us walk any faster. We were hungry and thirsty, and I knew Alex's legs were as weak as mine at the moment.

"I think he feels bad he left us with our grandparents after our mom died. And now that Amelia is pregnant, that means he's never coming back or even coming to get us."

"So that's it, then."

"Yes, that's it. And Abuelo is pissed because he knows Apá will be asking for money from him and Abuela."

"What a shitty father," Alex said.

I didn't want to ask if he meant Apá or Abuelo or both. I didn't want to know. I didn't care. I was sleepy suddenly, and I began to fantasize about the college dormitory room I remembered from the brochure that awaited me in a year or so. It would be the first time I would have my own bed.

When we exited the blocks of grapevines, we were met with a breeze. It was refreshing and liberating. But there was no movement as far as the eye could see. And not much sound, except for the vibrations of the telephone cables above us.

"So what are you doing with your first check?" I said.

Alex smiled. "Buying our dad a car so he can get our asses to work. You?"

"Same thing."

"What about your fancy shoes?"

I shrugged. Fancy shoes seemed so useless all of a sudden. But a bicycle would have helped. I let out a laugh.

"What's so funny?" Alex asked.

"Nothing. I was just thinking that maybe you weren't wrong about the bicycle after all."

"I told you, stupid. You and your fancy-ass shoes. Where do you think you're going?"

The answer was complicated: I was going to leave eventually. I was going to leave him. But that didn't seem like the right moment to tell him. So I simply said, "Nowhere. I'm not going anywhere yet."

"That's right, Turrútut. Like it or not, we're stuck here together, you and me."

I had the strangest sensation that Alex was trying to tell me something, but I was too brain-dead. Or maybe I was reading too much into his words. Our father had abandoned us, but my leaving was not the same thing. And not for a few more years. Perhaps all he needed was reassurance. Especially after seeing our father break down in front of us.

"Hey, listen, Alex, it's going to be okay. I'll always be here for you. I promise."

Alex looked at me intently. We had to try to read each other's minds. Unlike Apá, he was not one to let his defenses down. We locked eyes for a few seconds, and then he turned away. We slipped into silence again. That was all the sentimentality we were going to manage between us.

No car passed us by for an additional thirty minutes, but we didn't have to wait any longer because the blue Mustang came speeding out of the dirt avenue kicking up dust. Our father honked the horn, and our bodies jumped with excitement.

"We got a jump from the foreman," Apá said. "He was making one last inspection, and your grandfather spotted him."

Abuelo raised his chin slightly, acting like the hero of the story.

I patted Abuelo on the shoulder in gratitude. "Good job, Abuelo!"

"And don't you dare stop anywhere, Apá, in case the car won't start again," Alex said.

"Yeah," I piled on.

"Listen to your sons. Listen to your sons," Abuelo said.

Alex and I climbed in, and we set off for home. I made eye contact with Apá through the rearview mirror for a fleeting moment. In the back seat, as we sat side by side, a glorious comfort came upon me, and I might have held my brother's hand if it weren't the least manly gesture of affection I could imagine. So instead I joined the banter and laughter until we reached the freeway, where we blended into the traffic, just one more anonymous unit of Mexicans in the desert. It felt good to be in the company of these men. For once, I felt I belonged to this private world we called manhood, which wasn't perfect, which was sometimes painful, but was my birthright.

Acknowledgments

Portions of this book have been published previously, appearing in earlier versions. I thank the editors of the following journals: *Apogee, Barzakh, Boiler Journal, Essay Daily, Florida Review, Jelly Bucket, Numéro Cinq, Prairie Schooner,* and *TriQuarterly.*

The title of this book is inspired by the Pablo Neruda line "la luz de junio ahogaba flores en tu boca" (the light of June drowned flowers in your mouth) (my translation) from the poem "Explico algunas cosas" ("I Explain Some Things").

Gratitude to the United States Artists foundation for a generous grant and to Rutgers-Newark, the State University of New Jersey, for a timely sabbatical—both gifts allowed me to live in Puerto Rico for three months to complete this book.

Love to my compadre Richard Yáñez and to my comadre Mahsa Hojjati for long-distance affection. Love to Eduardo C. Corral, Daniel Enrique Pérez, Dee Rees, and Sarah Broom for continued friendship.

LIVING OUT

Gay and Lesbian Autobiographies

David Bergman, Joan Larkin, and Raphael Kadushin
FOUNDING EDITORS

The Other Mother: A Lesbian's Fight for Her Daughter
Nancy Abrams

An Underground Life: Memoirs of a Gay Jew in Nazi Berlin
Gad Beck

Gay American Autobiography: Writings from Whitman to Sedaris
Edited by David Bergman

Surviving Madness: A Therapist's Own Story
Betty Berzon

*You're Not from Around Here, Are You? A Lesbian in Small-Town
America*
Louise A. Blum

In the Province of the Gods
Kenny Fries

Travels in a Gay Nation: Portraits of LGBTQ Americans
Philip Gambone

Autobiography of My Hungers
Rigoberto González

What Drowns the Flowers in Your Mouth: A Memoir
    of Brotherhood
Rigoberto González

Widescreen Dreams: Growing Up Gay at the Movies
Patrick E. Horrigan

The End of Being Known: A Memoir
Michael Klein

Through the Door of Life: A Jewish Journey between Genders
Joy Ladin

The Last Deployment: How a Gay, Hammer-Swinging Twentysomething
    Survived a Year in Iraq
Bronson Lemer

Eminent Maricones: Arenas, Lorca, Puig, and Me
Jaime Manrique

Body Blows: Six Performances
Tim Miller

1001 Beds: Performances, Essays, and Travels
Tim Miller

Cleopatra's Wedding Present: Travels through Syria
Robert Tewdwr Moss

*Good Night, Beloved Comrade: The Letters of Denton Welch
    to Eric Oliver*
Edited and with an introduction by Daniel J. Murtaugh

Taboo
Boyer Rickel

Secret Places: My Life in New York and New Guinea
Tobias Schneebaum

Wild Man
Tobias Schneebaum

Sex Talks to Girls: A Memoir
Maureen Seaton

Treehab: Tales from My Natural, Wild Life
Bob Smith

Outbound: Finding a Man, Sailing an Ocean
William Storandt

Given Up for You: A Memoir
Erin O. White